Genesis:

As It Is Written

Genesis: As It Is Written

Contemporary Writers on Our First Stories

Edited and Introduced
by David Rosenberg

 HarperSanFrancisco
An Imprint of HarperCollins*Publishers*

| A TREE CLAUSE BOOK |

HarperSanFrancisco and the editor, in association with The Basic Foundation, a not-for-profit organization whose primary mission is reforestation, will facilitate the planting of four trees for every one tree used in the manufacture of this book.

FIRST EDITION

Library of Congress Cataloging-in-Publication Data

Genesis: as it is written : contemporary writers on our first stories / edited and introduced by David Rosenberg.—1st ed.
    Includes bibliographical references.
    ISBN 0–06–066706–0 (cloth)
    ISBN 0–06–066736–2 (pbk.)
    1. Bible. O.T. Genesis—Criticism, interpretation, etc.
    2. Bible as literature. I. Rosenberg, David.
    BS1235.2.G385 1996   96–22427
    222'.1106—dc20

96 97 98 99 00 ❖ RRD(H) 10 9 8 7 6 5 4 3 2 1

Contents

Acknowledgments

"Go beyond the art of Genesis and face its authors," I answered, when asked what new dimension these writers might add. My interlocutor was John Loudon, executive editor of HarperSanFrancisco, and his austere response—"do it"—gave life to this book. Lew Grimes, the most intrepid of literary agents, made that conversation possible.

The careful handling of Karen Levine, editor, was a privilege to be near, while the voice of Peter Evers in publicity was unusually sensible.

Dr. David Lee, of Florida International University, kept all of Florida's libraries open to me. The poet Leonard Schwartz kept me thinking. The editorial help of novelist Barbara Rogan was indispensible back at the origins of imagining writers with Bibles.

My mother, Shifra Asarch of Coconut Creek, was the guardian of optimism, aided by my mother-in-law, Wanda Ramby of Houston. My wife, Rhonda, as always, was everything.

—David Rosenberg

Introduction:
As It Is Written

David Rosenberg

The writers of Genesis must have brought pride in a heroic imagination to their Hebraic culture. But today, tradition keeps us confined to the commentators who came after and who inflated the meaning of the text. The novelists and poets who have come together in this book are of a different cast of mind: they remain open to the motivations and voices of the original authors. The writers in *Genesis: As It Is Written* are aware of the masks of selfhood that all authors wear. By mirroring their ancient counterparts, our imaginative writers today surpass the conventional commentators. The latter, such as those chosen for Bill Moyers's Genesis TV series, are wedded to ideas about the text that keep the original authors from memory.

The Authors, Then and Now

"I can't write an article anymore," said Isaac Bashevis Singer in his eighties, "but I can give you an interview." I had asked Singer to write the essay on Genesis for *Congregation* (1987), the first book I edited on writers and the Bible. Several tape-recorded interviews later—Singer with Hebrew Bible in his lap—I edited myself out and whittled down the typescript to the required personal essay. I was excited that it sounded more like Singer than any previous memoir (all his nonfiction was memoir). It had the pungent Yiddish wit and inflection of his speech, and I looked forward to his praise.

"It's awful. I would never write anything like that," he told me over the phone. "You cannot use it." I was at a loss for words. Then he continued, "But I was so ashamed of it that I wrote you an article like you asked." So I would have the author himself and not a redacted oral chronicle—and that was far better, no matter how highly I thought of my editorial skills. In a similar manner, it is the minds and sensibilities of the Bible's original authors—not their archaic oral sources—that I have asked today's novelists and poets to divine. The time has come to replace the antiquated notion of a Bible put together by scribes from oral shamans, or a Genesis in the image of its priestly redactor, piously applying scissors and paste. It has been obvious for some time that Genesis is too sophisticated for that. Yet the hold of religious and scholarly tradition remains strong, so that to imagine great Hebraic writers of independent mind, whose names remained known for centuries before the Babylonian exile, is resisted.

Where, however, is even the modern Yiddish culture that produced Isaac Bashevis Singer? It has been almost extinguished in our time. And by the days of the rabbis of antiquity, the Hebraic culture that produced Genesis ten centuries earlier was beyond recollection. It is as if we were to look back a century from now and determine that Singer's renderings of provincial Jewish life were tape-recorded "oral histories" rather than masterfully written stories. What we would gain in the sense of documentary history we would lose twice over by having lost hold of a great

Jewish sensibility and the cultures that shaped him. And just as Singer was influenced by the literature of many cultures—by Dostoyevsky in Russian and Dickens in English, for example— the Bible's writers would have known many literatures from their region, as well as from the past.

It was the plan of *Genesis: As It Is Written* to bring together a community of writers that reflected the diversity of authors behind the Book of Genesis. In addition to the Jews, Catholics, and Protestants represented here, there are a variety of genres: writers of plays, stories, novels, poems, and essays. Many of the writers struggle to characterize a Genesis author, sometimes as sacred story writer, sometimes as ironic narrator. Without relying on the jargon of literary critics, each writer uses his or her own experience as a narrator to provide a link with the biblical author. Something distinctly new is offered: these writers read the Bible as authors who are sensitive to the dynamic act of writing. The crucial distinction between this personal reading and that of the Bible experts is one of unorthodox authority. The scholars describe the landscape of Genesis based on the text, while these writers actually enter the landscape and describe the emotional drama of its composition. For instance, in the book's closing essay, Robert Pinsky compares the *teller* of the Joseph story—who tells it in the persona of a "nurse or grandmother"—to the Genesis narrator who weaves the genre of folktale into her larger work of tragic dimensions, which points back to Jacob and forward to Moses. This Genesis narrator, in her poetic genius, is grounded in an autobiography, and instead of a personal autobiography, Pinsky emphasizes that it is the autobiography of a people. What is Pinsky's authority here? As a poet and translator himself, he knows that to translate Dante he must rely on his own practice as a poet, and that poetry is rooted in autobiography: he is Joseph the translator of dreams as well as the poet who wrote this portion of

Genesis. His practice as a writer allows him to identify with the Genesis author—a difficult thing for a scholar or critic to do, since their personal life is too often unexamined.

In the same way, Grace Schulman, whose essay opens the book, identifies the Creation poet among the many authors behind Genesis. By contrasting Caedmon, the first English poet, she heightens our awareness of how much we've lost in the erasure of the ancient Hebraic culture that produced the Bible's first writers, and of how much we continue to lose by failing to imagine it. Between these two essays, most of the authors in *Genesis: As It Is Written* take up their stance as novelists, poets, and essayists whose own work provides a modern mirror for the sensibilities of biblical writers. This is a unique congregation of Jew and non-Jew who have come together to read in this way. It may also be the most intimate reading the Book of Genesis has received. Maturity is the most consistent theme, along with an increasing awareness of the original Hebraic culture that is suppressed.

Where does this new vulnerability in the way writers read the Bible come from? It is in large measure due to the revival of Hebrew as a spoken and literary language in the twentieth century. The language becomes personal again, living in a way it never could in the hands of religious enthusiasts or academicians whose intentions are didactic. My own experience in Israel, beginning two decades ago, has been shared by other poets. After the exhilaration of my first translations of psalms, I flew to Tel Aviv. While I was there I was invited to appear on a television show, hosted by the avant-garde poet David Avidan (who died last year), to read my translations from the Bible.

That night I watched the guests preceding me on the dressing room monitor. One was a man who had survived a car-crash coma and described out-of-body experiences when he drove again. The others around me were laughing but I was not yet speaking Hebrew well enough to catch the irony. In

fact, I didn't quite catch Avidan's translations of my own psalm
translations, as he read them on the air. I tried to smile as I
heard some behind-the-camera chuckles. It was nevertheless a
revelation to me, this familial merriment about the Bible. Certainly it is sacred, they seemed to be saying, but it is family poetry and we know all its flaws.

Experiences like this helped me to define my own autobiographical voice among the Bible's authors. I'd been educated to
think the Bible was half the story of Western cultural origins; the
classical Greek and Latin was the other half. Yet I found a famil-
iarity with ancient Greek in the Hebrew Bible itself, as I came to
translate Ecclesiastes. This author, known as Qohelet in Hebrew,
had absorbed a great deal of Greek literature, and I started to
think of him as more modern than I'd expected. I began to find
throughout the Hebrew Bible an awareness of the larger world
and a cultivated irony in assimilating other literatures.

Qohelet put on the mask and speaking voice of King
Solomon with a modern tonality in the fourth century B.C.E. I
only followed in his footsteps when I made Solomon's voice
my own in my translation. Qohelet pictured King Solomon as
a poet and builder, a Renaissance man who embellished his literary career with gardens and vineyards; I modernized this
portrayal by giving Solomon a more prominent writing career
and returning to him all his attributed books. Solomon's feasts
became contemporary parties, his passions my own. I imagined nothing that the original author had not imagined in his
own way, but I made the Bible's music more personal—just as
Qohelet had made the old king in his own image, five centuries
after Solomon's death.

so I set to work

in the grand style
building an oeuvre
ten books in five years

works of love and despair
naked and shameless
I was married and divorced

I went to all the parties
the glittering eyes
and wit: passion-starved

a trail of blinding jewels
of experience behind me
more than any king in Jerusalem

I tried on every life-style
I pushed to the center
through many gaudy affairs

I was surrounded by stars
singers and dancers
and fresh young bodies

to choose among
at the slightest whim
I was high and I was courted

but I kept my sense of purpose. . . .

In our time, after almost a century of modern literary and Hebrew studies, the Jewish way of reading the Bible imaginatively has been absorbed. It illuminates issues that are only hinted at by the specialist—issues of origins, inspiration, vision, irony, and repression. Today, the contributors to *Genesis: As It Is Written* illustrate the force of individual response and the necessity of imaginative growth. By insisting upon how it was written, many of these writers suggest how the authors of the Bible, like great writers in other cultures, are creators of consciousness. Writers as disparate as Alfred Corn and Norma Rosen suggest that the original biblical writers were creating midrash or commentary for even earlier books that are lost, just as the later books of the Prophets fulfill that role for the Genesis writers. Why, then, does history remember only the later traditions of the rabbis and saints, and not the writers?

The answer will become apparent in these essays, which are so rooted in the secular culture that they suggest the Bible's original writers were more secular than religious themselves. They were also readers, though we have lost the libraries of their day. Too often, conventional readings avoid the humanity of the authors and emphasize the biblical characters within the text instead. So *Genesis: As It Is Written* is a work of cultural outreach in this sense: it breaks down the barriers between religious and secular cultures—barriers that probably didn't exist in the biblical writers' day.

The First Audience

Was the Book of Genesis written to be read aloud? And if not, who were its original readers? Learned in languages and scripts, these first readers were most likely writers themselves, for whom the texts and stories of their culture needed to be retranslated from cuneiform script into the current idiom. There were probably many different idioms and strategies to the telling that are lost to us—and many stories that are lost as well. But what made this early biblical culture a renaissance was its maturity, its ability to retell the stories with a heightened sense of the individual reader. And the model of that reader was a professional writer at the Davidic or Solomonic courts in the tenth century B.C.E.

If "a dispassionate eye is the condition of a compassionate intelligence," as Simon Schama writes of Flaubert, then the Genesis writers are our masters. Some editorialize a bit, but unlike conventional religious writers, they impose no lessons on the reader: these were readers who had too much compassion for what was lost. It could only have been an ancient Hebraic renaissance that made such compassion for figures of the distant past, an Eve or a Rachel, indispensable. In the same way that ancient Hebraic writers used their past, the writers in this book look back to Genesis as cultural bedrock that their own works renew—not in a common culture (except perhaps among Israeli writers) but as individuals.

The early biblical writers probably had a more sophisticated audience than authors today: the Solomonic court was seasoned with fellow writers, translators, and scholars. The conventions of Hebrew storytelling were variations of those in Canaanite cultures, yet each writer had his or her own way to surprise the audience with unexpected divergence, to hold its attention. This professional audience would not have been moved by over-embellishment or virtuosity. Instead, we have received a powerful and uncanny narrative precisely because its audience demanded it. This was a reading audience, not one that was read to. It was different than most audiences today, including the first one I came to know as a child actor in radio. Here was a sophisticated illusion of oral storytelling as I'd known it as a child, from written scripts; and in the same manner, religious audiences, which came long after the first readers, took in the Bible by ear and became detached from the text's origins.

I was a regular on the weekly program "Honor the Name." Each episode told the life of a mythic American personage lending his name to a Detroit school. I played the patriarch in his youth—Franklin, Mumford, even Statler. The honored convention: each week our hero rose from humble beginnings. Then came the week of Clara Barton, and with no young girl present I began to realize I would be playing this role as well, in my pre-adolescent falsetto. Just be myself, I was told. I was and wasn't. Then a mature woman's voice took over the older Nurse Barton, and only to me did it seem uncanny. The first biblical

audience of highly educated readers would have scorned the
program—no canny directors and stale conventions for them.
Let's portray Sarai annoying God with laughter, they would
have suggested, and Abram haggling with God and winning his
point. Let's portray Tamar seducing her father-in-law Judah in
God's name. And as Leonard Michaels informs us in his ardent
essay, the complexity of this story is bound up with the creative
maturity of its author.

Consider the text of Genesis: where do Adam and Eve come
from, figuratively? The cultural context for their origins is
missing because we have not attempted to reimagine the Hebraic culture that borrowed and shaped them. The libraries of
the Davidic and Solomonic renaissance are lost to us, along
with their sense of the individual represented by his art: his
sense of distance from and irony toward the myth of his day
and toward convention (only lesser writers identify fully with
the conventional). We can, however, imagine the loss by con-
sulting our own culture of writers today, to see how convention works in them and how they may withstand it. Most
crucially, we can watch them restore a lost culture as they read
its texts from within their lives, and beyond simply their pro-
fessions. In this way, *Genesis: As It Is Written* unfolds a story of
leading writers in America as well. They are students or layper-
sons in the best sense, much like their readers. In *Congregation,*
Singer had written: "I am still learning the art of writing from
the Book of Genesis." Now the writer's creative process can
provide a necessary analogy for restoring the living quality
of Genesis.

What is unique about reading the text *as it is written?* Those
words—*as it is written*—convey a biblical authority, a prece-
dent, in the life of a people, just as a writer today might say,
That's how it was, referring to personal events in his own life.
What is the standard of truth for such a story of the past? For a
writer it is a faith, a fidelity, to objective reality, whether in the

world of experience or in the inner world of feeling. The full
attention of the writer recognizes the other as himself: first in
the others of one's common culture, and then in the individual. As is becoming clear, the writers who wrote the foundation of Genesis were individuals whose names are lost.
Religion may imagine them martyrs to piety, but martyrs do
not write great stories. No, they were great *readers* first, as we
know from evidence of the library and archives at David's
palace, before there was even a stone laid for the Temple. The
scrolls and tablets there were read in silence by individuals—
not out loud in the anachronistic image. These readers were
writers themselves who could read several scripts, including
many languages in cuneiform. They knew the work of other
cultures and of their own past. The events they wrote about
were already distant, a time of great poignancy that had been
lost and needed to be reimagined.

Now in our time we have lost the power to imagine this
great culture. It is to imaginative writers again we may turn,
since the best among them are not swayed by a rush to relevance in place of an advance toward masterful art.

The Push and Shove of Relevance

Can we talk about ethics and ideology in Genesis? Yes, just as
we could in Shakespeare's *Hamlet* or any complex work of literature. But what came first, the great stories and poetry or the
didactic lessons? Scholarship shows it is the writers who came
first, while the didactic elucidators came later as simplifiers—
just as the various creeds of Judaism and Christianity today
need to hold to a simplified interpretation in order to support
their beliefs. The writers in *Genesis: As It Is Written*, however,
evoke a unique complexity that touches the original authors, as
their lives are interwoven with tales, with fiction and fact,
memory, and laws broken.

Many of the writers, Jewish and non-Jewish alike, refer
to the rabbis of the Midrash, whose playful use of words "exploits every scriptural pun it finds or half-creates," as Geoffrey
Hartman has written. Beyond this, Genesis is compared to
a range of Western authors that takes in the Orphic poets,
Spinoza, Samuel Beckett, Caedmon, Shakespeare, Jane Austen,
Giordano Bruno, Coleridge, Dante, Freud, Kierkegaard,
Harold Bloom, Lorca, Thomas Mann, and Tolstoy.

Conventional wisdom tends to forget that what was superstition until recently is mirrored by the new superstitions we live by. "Comets used to be feared. People believed that they would bring disaster, such as war or famine," instructs the TV news. And in a few centuries, after life is discovered on another planet, they will write about our time, "People still believed that life originated on earth." Perhaps the conventional interpretations of Genesis will then stand further exposed as repressions of the complexity of the original authors, and in particular the independence of mind of a great writer, to whom convention and superstition are always subject.

Meanwhile, the conventional experts will talk about why Genesis is special—but not about why it was written. Why, for instance, is a novel by Lore Segal or a play by Arthur Miller written? The question interrogates our culture, not just the individual, while its counterpart—the Hebraic culture that produced Genesis—is under a taboo of silence. When our most sensitive writers begin to reimagine it we will truly have our questions revivified. Meanwhile, our prominent explainers talk to us about morals and meanings and messages, unconcerned about self-righteous poses. Yet many of the authors here put forward these popular explanations, from the rabbis to the TV, and show why they are largely wrong. Our foundational stories for Western culture were not written to explain anything; they were written to dramatize the creative blessings inherent in a marriage of mind and sensibility, a cultural union of secular and divine.

It is one thing to say that we have lost the original meaning of the poet and thus the power of images such as "sheaves bowing down." It is another to understand that we must restore this original vitality. Today there is an openness to restoration, whether it be of degraded ecosystems or endangered cultures. But this is not reflected by the popular media, where a passion for relevance and journalistic meaning smothers the elusive imagination. Even Bill Moyers's *Genesis* program on PBS, wanting to choose the brightest minds in the field, tended to choose only the most conventional ones, those who rush to relevance. What the writers in this book take for granted, on the other hand, are not the words but the greatness of the imagination behind them. Referring to Jacob's encounter with an angel, Edward Hirsch writes, "The Yahwist [or J, the earliest author of Genesis] who dramatized this episode, perhaps some time around the tenth century B.C.E., was first and foremost not a theologian but a lyricist and a storyteller." What the writers in *Genesis: As It Is Written* value is not relevance but the love for great literature that animated the original authors. That is why their first imaginative task is often to walk in the shoes of those authors. As the critic Helen Vendler wrote about the poet Robert Lowell when he taught the poets of the past, including the Greek poets contemporaneous with the biblical, Hebraic ones, "he knew them from their writing better than most of us know others from life." He gave to his students "the sense, so absent from textbook headnotes, of a life, a spirit, a mind, and a set of occasions from which writing issues—a real life, a real mind, fixed in historical circumstances."

Hearing, Writing, Translating

As the junior congregation's cantor at age twelve, I related to the boys and girls fidgeting in their seats, but in my responsibilities as cantor I had to restrain myself in my chair on the *bimah* (or dais) and listen to the children's sermon delivered by our mentor, "Sexton Ralph." Abram smashed his father's idols, according to one. And how was he punished by his angry father? According to Sexton Ralph's quotation of the Midrash, he was banished from home, sent "'out of his father's house,' as it is written." To me, it sounded like an adventure, not punishment. I understood that *that* was literature: even tragedy was an adventure, holding a complex point of view beyond any moral or lesson derived from it, as I had discovered in the *David Copperfield* I was reading.

A typical need of the conventional explainers, who present Genesis as written by religious committee over the ages, is to make Abraham monotheistic when he is not. "The patriarchs never appear as reproaching their contemporaries for idolatry," wrote the Israeli historian Yehezkel Kaufman. "Indeed, there is no religious contrast between the patriarchs and their surroundings." The idol-smashing rabbinical commentary about Abram's youth is a lesson in youth rebellion, and it is also the portent of a writer: Abram's journey to Canaan represents the process of outward adventure and inner resistance to the past. But the fact in the biblical story, as J presents it in Genesis, is that Abram's father left Canaan, with Abram in tow. What call did his *father* answer to "go forth"? Only after his father has died does Abram hear a call, the grandiosity of a new father speaking to him. This one represents God speaking to a historical man for the first time. In place of his real father, the blessing Abram receives suggests a double burden, a price for being different: the "go forth" he accepts is the solitude of the individual acquiescing in a process of a father's journey that remains unfinished. As James Carroll suggests in his essay here, it is the writer's journey as well, to an unforeseen closure—to be surpassed by further books, further children, and the memory of ancestors.

In my early forties, after more than a decade of translating other books of the Hebrew Bible, I began to translate the J

writer of Genesis. The wonder of the tales themselves, the
self-conscious telling by the narrator in her unconventional
puns and irony, indicated a tale retold not for moral purposes
but in the cultural pride of lived experience, and in its wisdom: conventional tales turned into unconventional stories, a
written art. My own earliest memory involves asking my
mother to "tell me a story." Not just asking—a crying need, to
fend off the dark. After a while the stories repeat and become
rote, are told the same, and with the same dramatic emphases.
But in a written text all can change. I found in adolescence I
could read it *my* way, follow my own sense of adventure, savor
a scene or pause at the brink somewhere. I could make it personal, invoking my own experiences; I could walk in the shoes
of the author.

There is still only one translation that puts us in mind of the
original authors. The current attempts to dislodge the authority of the King James translation of the Bible, by new translators on the left and new simplifiers on the right, has succeeded,
until it is writers themselves who must come to the rescue. In
the only writerly translation we have—for the King James is
the only one in which a reader can believe that great writers
were at work—a dynamic culture of writers in the Elizabethan
Renaissance paralleled the Solomonic court of biblical authors.
The writers in *Genesis: As It Is Written* mostly prefer the King
James for this reason. Consider this analogy: in an interview
with Sam Donaldson of ABC during Pat Buchanan's primary
campaign, Buchanan said, "Listen, Sam, you may believe you're
descended from monkeys. I don't believe it. I think you're a
creature of God." Unfortunately for us, the "monkeys" here
might stand as well for the original Hebraic writers of Genesis
and their continued suppression as writers, rather than as
saints or scribes. The writers here might reply that they believe
they were descended from writers, and do not wish to forget it.

The Story of the
Creation Poet

Grace Schulman

"In the beginning, God created the heaven and the earth." So opens the story in which God calls into being light, land and sea, fish, animals, men and women. These are verses of pure wonder, and the tone is achieved paradoxically by the negation of wonder. The God that is known through his words has a voice that is never heard directly—and that is its power. The narrator of this mightiest of all deeds is a recorder whose modesty ironically heightens the drama. The account is set forth simply and clearly, with an unexpected bareness of utterance. The poet has muted personal emotion to emphasize the miracle of God's handiwork, the force of God's supreme commands, and the speed with which they are fulfilled: "And God said, Let there be light: and there was light."

The poet's artistry is staggering. The evaluation that follows God's creation of light, "And God saw the light, that it was good," certainly is meiotic, or ironically understated. Although "good" has a greater range of meaning in the Hebrew of Genesis than in English, it is still in the subdued narrator's tone. But the understatement changes to marvel when it is used as a refrain, "And God saw that it was good . . ." occurring five times at the ends of verses and varied in the first chapter's final verse: "And God saw every thing he made, and behold, it was very good." Further, "it was good" alternates with "it was so," both accenting the jobs done swiftly and well. Those repetitions build throughout the passage. They grow louder, characterizing the narrator as not simply detached but controlled. Finally, he is filled with pent-up emotion. God is pleased; the narrator is astonished. The image of Creation is made to shine forth with feelings that remain unspoken.

The process of Creation is mysterious. Elsewhere in Genesis, God's technical instructions are precise: Noah's ark, for example, is made of gopher wood, is three hundred cubits in length, three stories high, with a skylight and a side entrance (6:14–16). Here, though, God speaks, names, and, without further effort or blueprint, "it was so." In the only passage when God announces what is to come, "Let us make man in our own image," the intention is expanded, even glorified, with the addition of "after our likeness," emphasizing the holiness of "image" and implying the intended legacy of godly purity. Directly after those words, God gives man and woman custody of the earth and of all things in it.

That dexterity is found throughout the brief passage. Overall, there is a pleasing formal symmetry: Creation's six-day process is divided into two groups, the first of the elements, the second of those using them. In each three-day group, the first day has a single deed (light, heavenly lights); the second has a deed split into two parts (heaven and earth; birds and fish); the third has two distinct creations (dry land and sea; animals and human beings). By the first three verses of chapter 2 ("and God blessed the seventh day") God is delighted and exhausted. This is the last, and best, of the many worlds God has created and thrown away—310, according to legend.

God, the foremost artist, is an inveterate reviser. So must be the Creation poet.

To dramatize God's rule, the poet juxtaposes such great opposites as heaven and earth, morning and evening, day and night. The writer's musical effects—refrains, parallelisms, and repetitive parallelisms—start here and resonate throughout the Hebrew Bible. Recurrences of "it was good" and "it was so" are interspersed with another refrain, "And the evening and the morning were the first day," the number varying with each repetition.

The theme of fecundity is strengthened by parallels, or phrases in which like images glorify abundance: "And the earth brought forth grass, and herb yielding seed after its kind, and the tree yielding fruit, whose seed was in itself." It is further emphasized by repetitive parallels, or those same phrases made to recur, resulting in lines crowded with strong, persistent images. These bolster God's creation of the foliage and, later, of the animals:

> And God said, Let the earth bring forth the living creature after his kind, cattle, and creeping thing, and beast of the earth after his kind. . . . And God made the beast of the earth after his kind, and cattle after their kind, and every thing that creepeth upon the earth after his kind: and God saw that it was good.

By far God's highest blessing is fertility. Throughout the Hebrew Bible the theme returns: life after our kind is our immortality. Over and again, vital figures gain, are cheated of, and regain the right to extend their lives through progeny and more progeny. In the Creation story, God instructs creatures to continue life's ongoing beauty. It is merely an expectation for the fruit tree "yielding fruit, whose seed was in itself, after his kind." For fish, birds, and human beings, it is a divine award: "Be fruitful, and multiply, and fill the waters of the seas," and the gift is intensified by the device of parallelism.

"Be fruitful and multiply," the initial words of God's command to the fish and the birds, is repeated in the order to men and women. In contrast, though, God's blessing on men and women follows directly the creation of man "in our own image." Moreover, when God exhorts human beings to be fertile and increase, the charge accompanies additional obligations—namely, the subordination of all other living things. Although the command seems shocking in our time, it assumes the model conduct of an untarnished prelapsarian world. I read the passage now for an ironic awareness that godly perfection is achieved only by the supreme being:

> And God blessed them, and God said unto them, Be fruitful, and multiply, and replenish the earth, and subdue it: and have dominion over the fish of the sea, and over the fowl of the air, and over every living thing that moveth upon the earth.

———————

My own enchantment with the Creation story began when I read of Caedmon, the elderly untaught farmhand who became our first poet. Caedmon's "Hymn," the first poem in English, is about the Creation. Caedmon's story is told by Bede, an eighth-century English historian who wrote mostly in Latin. Bede narrated miracles as well as historical facts, both in precise detail.

Caedmon worked in the fields near Whitby Abbey, a setting that matches the strangeness of this story. The abbey, when I visited it, was lodged high on a moor in Yorkshire, not far from the sea. To walk those heather-filled craters is to lose one's way, look up at dizzying horizons, and see, in that lunar country, the windowless skull that was Whitby. And even if Whitby has changed since seventh-century England, certain remarkable things remain: for one thing, there were those wild moors in which Caedmon perceived order; for another, Whitby was one

of the double monasteries of men and women that marked the
Anglo-Saxon Church. Hild, a woman, was abbess.

By nature, Caedmon resembles the restrained narrator of
the Creation story. Unable to learn verses, too shy to sing at a
feast where guests were required to improvise, Caedmon fled
to a barn to care for the horses. He fell asleep and dreamed "a
person" commanded him to sing the origin of things. On waking, he remembered the dream words:

> Nu sculon herigean   heofonrices weard
> metodes meahte   and his modgethanc
> weorc wuldoraedor   swa he wundra gehæs
>
> Now we shall praise   heaven's keeper
> the maker's might   and his mind's thought
> father of the world   as of all wonder . . .

That is the opening of Caedmon's "Hymn." When the
Abbess Hild heard of it, she invited Caedmon to instruct the
monks in prayer. Thereafter, he continued to write verses that
suited the monastery, modeling his language on the war songs
of the royal meadhalls. Bede's account—that "someone," presumably an angel, commanded Caedmon to sing—always
struck me as the human tendency to find a concrete reason for
the artist's power, that eludes reason.

Caedmon's method bears watching. He writes of God's Creation in Anglo-Saxon, the language of a pagan culture. The
creation story Caedmon had known was in the Bible translation of his time, Saint Jerome's fourth-century Vulgate text.
The poems he had heard were the monks' Latin prayer chants
at Whitby, and, in contrast, the battle songs sung by scops, or
local bards, about the warlords they served.

In his Creation hymn, Caedmon used the scops' epithets
for king: "keeper," "ruler," "lord." At the same time, he used
adjectives ("heaven," "lord") to qualify the epithets. Had he,

in reverse, sung of war in Latin, he would not have been the first English poet. Indeed, the result might have ranged from mediocrity to disaster. Instead, he composed his great new song by fusing the rock-hard, brawny *language* of war with the noble *matter* of God's Creation. Throughout literature we find masterful ways of combining sacred and secular, doctrine and language, such as, for example, Dante's use of the vernacular for his sacred subject. It strikes me here that Caedmon was alert to the sameness, rather than the differences, of the two cultures, by combining pictures and words. To depict Creation, he uses "maker" and "father" as marvelous puns. He plays with language: if king is lord, then God is King; if king is keeper, then God is heaven's keeper.

The Anglo-Saxon poet's story reminds me of my grandfather's musical practice. A Hungarian Jew, he was a lawyer who sang for his father, a cantor in a synagogue in New York's lower East Side. My grandfather sang the liturgy to tunes he had heard in music halls. His favorite tune, "There's *one* New York, there is but *one* New York," was sung by a woman named Bessie, who wore tights; to this melody he fit the Sabbath prayer's words, "Le *ha* dodi le *krat* shalat," based on the Song of Solomon. What he did was at least another step in the ongoing aesthetic process of transforming the liturgy and popular culture.

Caedmon's hymn is central to my life. I memorized it when, during a hiatus between college and graduate school, I worked as a newspaper reporter covering a police beat on a northern Virginia daily. My notes on current events were immediate, urgent—and transient. So much for the present. I longed to read literature of the past, which would leave an indelible mark on the future.

In that dislocation, after a long silence, I wrote of Caedmon and his hymn. In my poem, Hild overheard him sing and, knowing he was uneducated, attributed his inspiration to an

angel's visit. I imagined Caedmon leaving a banquet where the
gleemen sang battle songs of the kings they served. Too shy to
perform there, he fled to a barn and sang the Creation. My
poem, "The Abbess of Whitby," collected in *Burn Down the*
Icons, opens with Hild's exclamation:

> There must have been an angel at his ear
> When Caedmon gathered up his praise and sang,
> Trembling in a barn, of the beginning,
> Startled at words he never knew were there. . . .

More recently, I've been drawn to *Bereshit,* the Hebrew
name for Genesis. Literally meaning "At the beginning of," it
comprises the first words of the text. The word is magical, for
it implies all origins. One of the poems in my latest book—
"God's Letters," in *For That Day Only*—was inspired by possibly prebiblical legends that informed the Creation poet:

> When God thought up the world,
> the alphabet letters
> whistled in his crown,
> where they were engraved
> with a pen of fire,
> each wanting to begin
> the story of Creation. . . .

The Creation poet is the unacknowledged master of inte-
grating the sacred and the secular, using the legends and languages of at least two cultures. The Hebrew Genesis bears a
startling resemblance to an earlier Babylonian epic, *enuma
elish,* or "When on High." In fact, the two texts share precise
details. E. A. Speiser, whose translation of Genesis appears in
the Anchor Bible, points out that the order of events is the
same in both texts, a fact that argues for the Hebrew having
borrowed from the Mesopotamian source. In both accounts,
the sequence is divine spirit; chaos and darkness; the creations

of light, firmament, dry land, luminaries, man. The crucial difference is that in the Babylonian epic, everything emanates from the gods, and on the seventh day the gods rwest and celebrate. In the Hebrew Bible, there is one God.

Where Caedmon uses biblical myth for his Anglo-Saxon hymn, the Creation poet writes in Hebrew, using the details of the Babylonian cosmic legend and a monotheistic God. Both Caedmon and the Creation poet are attentive less to the differences between cultures and doctrines than to the images they share—Caedmon's God as King arises from biblical myth plus the Anglo-Saxon kings and gods; the Creation poet's array of images and the idea of divinity are used to sing one God.

The Creation story tells of goodness everywhere. The stability of the single God—as opposed to the capriciousness of the many gods—has to do with that perfection. Later in Genesis, there will be evil. After the fall from Eden, which was based on deliberate choice, God's selection process narrows gradually, from Noah who is saved and Shem who is blessed to Abraham who is elect and Isaac who is chosen. Here at the start, though, there is universal justice and order.

For me, the single God that distinguishes the Hebrew Bible from the version or versions that preceded it signifies the single consciousness required by a work of art. The Creation is an image of the exemplary artist who lives, in Frost's words, "by turning to fresh tasks," making what will never be undone. He examines the raw material and shapes it—"the dry land," "the evening and the morning," "the tree yielding fruit"—then transforms it by commanding the work into being. It is done. He is pleased and somewhat startled by what is there. And the figure is presented by a poet who, after a long silence, awakens and sees things once deemed ordinary as miracles.

The Story of the Days of Creation

Madison Smartt Bell

Some years ago, around the first of May, I stopped working altogether for the first time in what then seemed a very long time. I'd spent a busy year teaching at the Iowa Writers' Workshop, and at around the same time I had finished a long novel—at semester's end, novel's end, I dropped as if my strings had been cut into a deck chair in the backyard of the house we were renting in Iowa City. I lay there for four days, doing nothing, in a sort of stunned silence, as if I had just awakened from a long strange dream and no longer had any standing rapport with reality. Reality then was an ancient, enormous apple tree, spreading its full spring bloom over the chair where I lay; when the wind blew, it would shower fragrant curling white petals over my knees and the overgrown grass like snow, and meanwhile seeds from the uncut dandelions rode their intricate feathering through the shafts of sunlight divided by the branches of the tree. I stared at the details of the scene with the kind of mute awe permitted by extreme exhaustion. The shape of apple petals, the design of dandelion seeds . . . all such small matters seemed of the utmost significance. I felt, indeed, that they were sent to signify something to me.

In the beginning God created the heaven and the earth.

And the earth was without form, and void; and darkness was upon the face of the deep. And the Spirit of God moved upon the face of the waters.

And God said, Let there be light: and there was light.

And God saw the light, that it was good: and God divided the light from the darkness.

These first verses of Genesis have always held a fascination for writers because of their assertion of the power of the word. It is God's speech that brings the first things into being, His omnipotently creative word. As God commands, so things become, and in Genesis, creation is an authoritative act, not to say authoritarian—but in either case this version of events has often been taken as a reassuring confirmation of the powers assumed by authors.

But, that halcyon May in Iowa, I began to blunder toward a different way of thinking about Creation, beginning with that familiar Romantic preoccupation that in the bloom of any flower lie thoughts too deep for dreaming. As it happened, I had a book to read while I reclined beneath the apple tree: *Giordano Bruno and the Hermetic Tradition,* by Frances Yates. I was reading it for no particular purpose, but it soon struck me that Bruno's appropriation of the *Corpus Hermeticum* provided a complete cosmological explanation for the apple blossoms and dandelion seeds and also for the essential fascination with such things that had for the moment overtaken me.

Giordano Bruno's elaborate cosmology is founded on a technical mistake common to his period: it was believed by many Renaissance mystics and even by some Christian theologians (Bruno himself was a renegade monk) that the *Corpus Hermeticum,* a body of first-century gnostic writings attributed to the mythic personage of Hermes Trismegistus, belonged to the culture of ancient Egypt. According to this error, the *Corpus Hermeticum* predates the Old Testament, and it becomes possible to think of Hermes Trismegistus as a pagan figure who in some ways prefigures Moses—as his supposed writings prefigure the Old Testament. Therefore when Giordano Bruno began adapting Hermetic lore for his own purposes, he believed that he was returning to the deepest original roots of the Judeo-Christian tradition.

The Renaissance version of Hermeticism espoused and to some extent invented by Giordano Bruno and others is a magical "religion of the world" founded on the principle of universal animism. The world, indeed the universe, is alive, and all its parts are therefore in animated correspondence with one another, like the parts of any living organism. (Here one finds some significant prefiguring of the New Age philosophical spin-offs from Lovelock's Gaia hypothesis.) Because of this infinitely extended relatedness of the Hermetic cosmology, it is possible by grasping any part of Creation (apple blossoms, dandelion seeds) also to grasp the whole. God, as has elsewhere been proposed, is fully immanent in each detail.

Giordano Bruno's "Memory Theater" is designed (among other things) to express this relatedness schematically. The Memory Theater takes the pattern of the pre-Copernican universe, with earth at the center and the belt of the zodiac surrounding it. This great circle is divided into pie wedges that emanate from the earth to the sea of divinity in which it floats—so that in principle every stone, twig, or mote of dust on earth can ultimately be traced back to its home with the divine. Renaissance Hermeticism is an optimistic mode of gnosis, and Bruno's Memory Theater was a device that, he believed, would make him omniscient once he had completely mastered it. In the Brunian model of the cosmos, omniscience and omnipotence are much the same thing.

Bruno (who lived in an age of monstrously destructive religious warfare) came to believe that Christianity had erred from its roots (roots that he thought were expressed by the *Corpus Hermeticum*). The mission of his life was to reform Christianity by teaching people (with all appropriate caution) that the divinity of Jesus Christ was not unique. As Christ is the Son of God, so are we all God's children, each of us equipped with a key to God's omniscience and omnipotence, if only we would learn how to make use of it. Thus the *imitatio Christi* (imitation of Christ) becomes an occult technique employing the things of this world (rather than transcending them, as in neoplatonism) as a sort of ladder whereby the adept ascends, bodily, into the divine realm as God's own equal.

Needless to say, this "reform" of orthodox Christian doctrine is heretical in the extreme. Giordano Bruno, who set out to become an international missionary for the new or old truths he had hit upon, also spent much of his life as an international fugitive. When the Inquisition finally overtook him, he was burned at the stake.

Nevertheless, Bruno's magical religion had a strong appeal for me as I lay there under the apple tree. The principle of universal animism, especially, seemed experientially true—it explained the strange potency that emanated from the petals and seeds blowing through the long grass. Was it not possible that the error of our way of being in the world began with our having failed to understand, or having forgotten, that the world itself is the body of God?

So I began to think about writing another novel. This book, published a few years later as *Doctor Sleep*, features an ex–drug addict American hypnotist living in London, who also happens to be a disciple of Bruno's mysticized *scientia*. This character, Adrian Strother by name, believes (among other very strange

things) that he can use self-hypnosis as an instrument for the
Brunian operation of reflecting the macrocosm of the universe
inwardly upon the microcosm of the mind—Bruno's method
for internalizing the Memory Theater in order to master all
the knowledge in the universe and render himself omniscient.
And like Bruno, my character is a cautious, covert proselyte for
the magical mystery that has explained the universe to him.

A document from the *Corpus Hermeticum* called *Pimander*
presents the Hermetic version of the creation myth, which
stands in an interesting and provocative relationship to the
creation story of Genesis 1. For the sake of comparison, the
Genesis version needs a longer, closer look.[1]

The beauty and majesty of its language and images are un-
mistakable and unforgettable. Because it is such a very well
known text, it may be at some risk of fading within its own fa-
miliarity, but a fresh and concentrated look shows that it is
burnished very bright. Above all the language is extremely
forceful; it reveals Yahweh in something close to his most awe-
full aspect—so that perhaps the majesty somewhat over-
whelms the beauty of the passage. There is a lot of subduing,
division, and dominion. Creation according to Genesis 1 is first
and foremost an expression of raw divine power, and God's all-
creating speech is here uttered in tones similar to the voice that
speaks to Job from out of the whirlwind.

Available English translations of the *Corpus Hermeticum* are
not very melodious (at least to my ear), so for the writing of
Doctor Sleep I used the translation into French by Festugière,
from the original Greek. The novel incorporates an extremely
freewheeling adaptation of Festugière's translation of *Pimander.*[2]

As a work of art, my rendering of *Pimander* can scarcely
stand up to the King James Version of Genesis (there's not
much in the English language that can). Furthermore, *Pimander* lacks the Genesis version's virtues of simplicity. In Genesis,
God's acts of creation are direct and straightforward, where in

Pimander those acts are encumbered by an almost-infinite recession of conceptually difficult, abstract mediation. But there are other differences between *Pimander* and the Genesis story that merit some consideration.

And at this point it might also be worthwhile to recall the real provenance of the *Corpus Hermeticum* (which Giordano Bruno and his *confrères* never knew)—that instead of predating the Old Testament, it comes after it, during the first century A.D.—co-evolving (together with other similar mystical doctrines) alongside the Christianity that would finally adapt itself and survive to become one of the world's greatest religions. With this in mind, a comparison of *Pimander* to Genesis suggests that the one is a reaction to the other—perhaps an attempted revision of the other. It may be that the unknown authors of the *Corpus Hermeticum* (for Hermes Trismegistus turns out to be a mythical figure who never really existed, in ancient Egyptian culture or anywhere else) had set out, as Bruno would do later, to reform the Judeo-Christian tradition from its Old Testament roots.

Creation according to Genesis is a story of separation and division. In the very beginning, God stands separate from the formless material from which the cosmos is to be made, and at the end, when His speech has divided everything into its proper category, God remains apart from His Creation and in some sense remote from it. But in *Pimander,* the emphasis is on union rather than division. At the level of divine origins, things cannot be told apart from one another; all is integrated and unified—and this unity is replicated in the nature of man, where it is said to be essential to man's animation. The first acts of Creation occur almost as parthenogenesis; God gives birth to the cosmos from within Himself. But the consummation of the Hermetic Creation is a human rather than a divine act, an act undertaken by man in his highly sexualized approach to "the beautiful body of Nature."

Almost everywhere that the Genesis story speaks of acts of power, the Hermetic myth of Creation speaks of acts of love. It is Love itself that completes Creation. The Fall is here rendered as a fall into corporeality, as in the more pessimistically gnostic neoplatonism, but where neoplatonism conceives of matter as an inanimate prison for the soul, in the Hermetic version matter is alive and full of potential to liberate the soul. In the Hermetic story, the fall into the body is expressed as a falling in love.

The division of creatures into the male and female sexes is thus consequent to the Fall as the Hermetic myth describes it. And the human longing for love may be translated as a longing for the divine state of origin, where the sexes are rejoined into the aboriginal whole. Properly understood, all human love can be translated into love for God—and according to the Hermetic fable, God remains available to receive and return this love. God is not divided or remote from His Creation as in Genesis, but fully immanent in every blossom and each seed.

Human error, as Giordano Bruno came to understand it, is explained by the fact that we have forgotten these truths; the soul's task is to relearn how to recognize them.

———————

As an educated citizen of the thoroughly secularized "First World," my hypnotist Adrian Strother inhabits a world much more catastrophically fallen than that portrayed by the initial Hermetic cosmology. Religion has been abandoned by most of the people in his sphere—to be inadequately replaced by one or another version of psychotherapy (of which he is himself a minor-league practitioner). Communities have collapsed, and families along with them. Rape, murder, and incest are prevalent everywhere. Love has been almost universally perverted into violence. It is painfully evident that something has gone very, very wrong. Somehow we have made a ruin of Creation.

The solution that Strother imagines is to reassert love as an emanation or immanence of the Divine. The great error of human beings (as Strother paraphrases Bruno) arises *"because they use force, and not love."* And in his effort to rectify this error, Strother follows Giordano Bruno along a path of gnosis that may very well lead to errors of its own.

Unquestionably, gnosis has its own set of hazards, and the version preferred by Giordano Bruno ultimately leads (among other things) to a cosmos dangerously overpopulated with omnipotent deities. But Bruno was right, I think, to observe that the principle of *caritas* had been lost from the orthodox practice of Christianity in his time. And certainly this principle seems to be quite generally absent from our lives today (inside or outside of conventional religious observance). Have we forgotten what it really means to say that God is Love? If so, it may be necessary to return to the first origins of Creation in order to regain our comprehension.

———————

1. In the beginning God created the heaven and the earth.

And the earth was without form, and void; and darkness was upon the face of the deep. And the Spirit of God moved upon the face of the waters.

And God said, Let there be light: and there was light.

And God saw the light, that it was good: and God divided the light from the darkness.

And God called the light Day, and the darkness he called Night. And the evening and the morning were the first day.

And God said, Let there be a firmament in the midst of the waters, and let it divide the waters from the waters.

And God made the firmament, and divided the waters which were under the firmament from the waters which were above the firmament: and it was so.

And God called the firmament Heaven. And the evening and
the morning were the second day.

And God said, Let the waters under the heaven be gathered together into one place, and let the dry land appear: and it was so.

And God called the dry land Earth; and the gathering together
of the waters called he Seas: and God saw that it was good.

And God said, Let the earth bring forth grass, the herb yielding
seed, and the fruit tree yielding fruit after its kind, whose seed is in
itself: and it was so.

And the earth brought forth grass and herb yielding seed after
his kind, and the tree yielding fruit, whose seed was in itself, after
its kind: and God saw that it was good.

And the evening and the morning were the third day.

And God said, Let there be lights in the firmament of the heaven
to divide the day from the night; and let them be for signs, and for
seasons, and for days, and years:

And let them be for lights in the firmament of the heaven to
give light upon the earth: and it was so.

And God made two great lights; the greater light to rule the day,
and the lesser light to rule the night; he made the stars also.

And God set them in the firmament of the heaven to give light
upon the earth,

And to rule over the day and over the night, and to divide the
light from the darkness: and God saw that it was good.

And the evening and the morning were the fourth day.

And God said, Let the waters bring forth abundantly the moving creature that hath life, and fowl that may fly above the earth in
the open firmament of heaven.

And God created great whales, and every living creature that
moveth, which the waters brought forth abundantly, after their kind,
and every winged fowl after his kind: and God saw that it was good.

And God blessed them, saying, Be fruitful, and multiply, and fill
the waters in the seas, and let fowl multiply in the earth.

And the evening and the morning were the fifth day.

And God said, Let the earth bring forth the living creature after his kind, cattle, and creeping thing, and beast of the earth after his kind: and it was so.

And God made the beast of the earth after his kind, and cattle after their kind and every thing that creepeth upon the earth after his kind, and God saw that it was good.

And God said, Let us make man in our image, after our likeness: and let them have dominion over the fish of the sea, and over the fowl of the air, and over the cattle and over all the earth, and over every creeping thing that creepeth upon the earth.

So God created man in his own image, in the image of God created he him, male and female created he them.

And God blessed them, and God said unto them, Be fruitful, and multiply and replenish the earth, and subdue it: and have dominion over the fish of the sea, and over the fowl of the air, and over every living thing that moveth upon the earth.

2. Hermes Trismegistus slept, his corporeal sense bound as by some heavy ligature, but his soul went gliding to the heights, and in the inspiration of his sleep a being called Pimander appeared to him. Pimander showed him a vision of a serene and joyful light; nothing was there but the limitless light, and the dreamer could not help but love it, but a vision of darkness followed it. The darkness of the infinite void became the very medium of Hermes Trismegistus's sleep, and the darkness turned in tortured spirals, like the body of a serpent. Then the darkness produced a vapor, like a fire, and it made an indescribable groan, like a cry of help from out of the fire. There was light again, and a holy Word written in the fire and leaping upward, and the air leapt upward after the fiery breath. Then the water and the earth appeared, intermingled so that one could not be told from the other, mixed in the moving breath of the Word.

That light, Pimander said, is I myself, Nous, thy God, and the luminous word issuing from the Nous is the Son of God. And that within you which watches and hears is the Word of the Lord, and your own spirit is God the Father; they may not be separated one from the other, because their union is life. Then fix your spirit on the light, and learn to know it well.

From the illuminated Word, Pimander said, next sprang the Demiurge, god of fire and of breath, to make the seven planets, Seven Governors each with its own powers, encircling one another in seven spheres, and the name of their government is destiny. The Word and the Demiurge combined themselves to cause the seven spheres to shudder and begin to move, and by reason of this movement the elements of the earth produced the animals who walk, and the air, the animals who fly, and the water, the animals who swim. And the elements sprang from the will of God, which was the maker of souls.

Then Nous, who was life and light, produced a Man like to himself, and loved him as a child. The Man was brother to the creative Demiurge and when he saw what his brother had made, he wished to make a work of his own. The Seven Governors became enamoured of him also, and they shared their powers with the Man, and taught him to know their essence and to participate in their being. Then the Man leaned down across the seven spheres, breaking through the envelopes that separated them one from another, and revealed the beautiful form of God to Nature. Seeing the inexhaustible beauty and energy of the Seven Governors joined to the form of God in Man, Nature smiled with love, for she had seen Man's marvelous beauty reflected brightly in the water of the oceans, and in Man's shadow covering the earth. Perceiving how it was like to himself, the Man fell in love with the beautiful body of Nature, and desiring to live with her, he entered the earth, so that he and the world were forged together in the heat of their love for one another.

Because of this movement, Pimander said, the nature of Man is always double. What had been Man's life became his soul, and his light became the intellect, and his body was like to the body of

Nature, reflecting it, but it was bound by mortality. And the Man, who was above the armature of the seven spheres, submitted himself to live beneath it, and submitted himself to the rule of destiny.

Turning in the darkness of his trance, Hermes Trismegistus longed to discover the path of liberation from this confinement, the way to reascend the seven spheres and return to his first home in the Divine. You are light and life, Pimander told him, like God the Father of whom Man was born. If therefore you learn to know yourself as made of light and life . . .

(*Doctor Sleep*, by Madison Smartt Bell. New York: Harcourt Brace, 1991. Pp. 191–92.)

The Story of
Adam and Eve

Arthur Miller

I first read Genesis—or parsed it out—in Hebrew, a language already associated in my mind with magic. I was six or seven years old and my translator was an ancient man with a long yellowed beard who smelled of strong snuff tobacco. I have never been good at memorizing and certainly wasn't then, especially Hebrew words. So I had to piece together, syllable by syllable, the creation of the world, gradually filling out the empty spaces like a jigsaw puzzle, and there was a certain suspense and therefore a kind of sensuality in the proceeding.

It was heavy duty—learning a language and simultaneously how the world was made, and the magical was inevitably a relief from having to figure it all out. The story itself was like any other story, authorless, self-generated, but extremely satisfying because it no sooner raised a question than it answered it. Did the world need light? God hung the stars and planets up like lanterns in the sky. How did Adam find a wife? God made her out of mist. The world before the Fall was like a wonderful painting hanging on the wall, and the story could have been written by a child for other children. In fact, its intense condensation is much like a cartoon, one discrete image following another, a quick and happy form of narrative.

But a certain darkness crept in with the appearance of the Mother. As a boy I was perfectly happy with Adam and God; now we had a woman to deal with, and mothers could see into a boy's mind and know what he was thinking, which was usually something bad. I was not absolutely surprised that Eve disobeyed and ate the apple and even got Adam to have a bite. This whole catastrophe takes one short paragraph, and there is no mention of the slightest hesitation on her or Adam's part. At this point it was not a pleasurable painting anymore but a battleground, and one where the issues were beyond me to understand. Yet the whole of Genesis remained in my imagination, filled as it was with mystery.

For one thing it is an amazing piece of prose—the whole world brought to such vivid life in a couple of pages. (I often think of its brevity when confronted by a six-pound novel.) But I think it lived on because it somehow held within it a secret, a key to some forgotten lock. It is as impenetrable as it is naive. Half a century later I would be moved to write a play based on Genesis in order to puzzle out its riddles.

I think the occasion for this play was the revolts of the Sixties, oddly enough. I was struck, even troubled, by a kind of echo of the Thirties, a time when I had come of age. This echo-effect lent a certain dream-like quality to the confrontations, almost as though they were being managed and controlled from deep under the ground by forces no one knew existed. For example, as an alumnus participant in some of the early anti-war sit-ins at the University of Michigan, where they began, I could fairly see and hear the fathers of some of the students before me demonstrating with very similar emotions against fascism, often in these very same buildings. The circularity of the repetition struck me when the Sixties students had

hardly any awareness that they were doing and feeling things
that others had felt and done in another age. And I couldn't
help wondering, at that high tide of idealism and outrage, how
they would manage their inevitable, if at the time unmention-
able, disillusionment. The Fall had to follow the Creation.

In this oblique way the Genesis story resumed its life in my
mind. But now it appeared to me as myth generated by strictly
human dilemmas that no human logic was able to rationalize.
It became the story of how man created God, but a god and a
cosmology that so beautifully answered to human needs that
he ended up being worshiped.

As written, Genesis describes a god quite unsentimental
about, if not totally unmindful, of justice, at least as ordinary
humans understand justice. In my play *The Creation of the
World and Other Business,* God is presented with offerings from
Cain and Abel. Of Abel's roast lamb: "Young man, this is un-
doubtedly the sweetest, most delicious, delicate, and profoundly
satisfying piece of meat I have ever tasted since the world began." The parents, of course, are ecstatic. "Boy," says Adam,
"this is our proudest moment." And Eve gives Abel a big kiss.

In the excitement they have all but forgotten Cain's offering.
"Lord," the boy says, "you haven't tasted my corn." And God
seals the fate of the world. "Oh, I can see it's all very nice. You
have done quite well, Cain. Keep it up."

Whatever the inspiration from above, a poet or poets wrote
Genesis, and some editor-rabbi made the decision to set it at
the very opening of the holy books of the Jewish people. It had
to be the first book because it tells why there has to be God,
and thus makes the rest of the Bible necessary. Without the
murder of Abel, the Bible is but one more clan history, a curio.
It is this fratricide that anchors the Jewish religion in human
life, just as the Crucifixion does in the Christian cosmos.

For if a brother could murder a brother, nobody is safe, all
bets are off, and there is no future. The act has to be condemned

absolutely and without the slightest hesitation or doubt. Thus God is brought down as the ultimate voice to drive Cain out of human society.

Playwrights are notoriously literal-minded, however. We have to be to manage human beings onstage. That God sends Cain out to be a vagabond in the land of Nod, east of Eden, is rather a shock to one who had believed, as the Bible said, that the First Family dwelt alone on the earth. Apparently there were already lots of other people just beyond the horizon, maybe even cities. So the Adam and Eve family were merely exemplars, poetic fictions drawn out of a humanity already on earth; the poet of poets simply gathered in his story the tensions of people living in an arbitrary, unjust world that ethically made no sense and morally had no existence. The god created in this story is still blind to injustice. To Cain, whose offering he gave "not respect," God has the nerve to ask, "Why art thou wroth? and why is thy countenance fallen?"

There was a joke in the Depression: a wealthy lady is confronted by a beggar who holds out his hand and says, "Lady, I haven't eaten in three days." To which she replies, "Well, you have to force yourself." The closest God comes to explaining his unequal treatment of the brothers is "If thou doest well shalt thou not be accepted?" Virtue, in short, is and has to be its own reward, for there can be no other, a veritable recipe for revolution.

To be sure this is honest; this is the way the world is; one man, for no discernible reason, gathers all the chips while the man next to him loses everything, including his self-respect. What can keep such a system from flying apart?

God, an extremely conservative gentleman, will keep it safe. For the poet-author knew the strength and weakness of the reed that is the axis of human society. In my play, Lucifer tries to keep Cain from killing his brother, explaining that the best way to frustrate the unjust God is to deprive Him of that

human guilt which drives men to their knees. "He has designed your vengeance, boy, he's boiling your blood in his
hand." Why?

> So He may stand above your crime, the blameless God,
> The only assurance of Mankind, and his power is safe.

And Cain is almost won by Lucifer's argument, until he
once again lays eyes on his always-fortunate brother, whereupon he cries out to heaven, "How is Abel the favorite of
God?" That cry of frustrated love is prelude to murder, and
Lucifer is forced to reveal his hidden agenda, his prescription
for his own ascent to the throne of the world. He tries to pull
Cain safely away from Abel, who is approaching. Cain cries
out, "I have to face him first!"

> *Lucifer:* Then face him with indifference.
> Kill love, Cain, kill whatever in you cares;
> Murder now is but another sort of praise to God!
> Don't praise him with a death! Indifference, Cain!

The play turned out—rather unexpectedly for me—to prove
love, as opposed to Luciferian indifference, the driving force
in Genesis. And the force, as well, driving the need of God's
moral adjudication; He may not exist in Heaven but he surely
does in the mind of man, if not as a ruling power then one to
bargain with.

I began thinking about the play as a casting of light upon the
rule of myths that seem so heaven-borne but spring from man's
commonest needs, and are his inventions. But at the end of the
day it seems hardly to matter whether God came from man or
man from God; an appeal to an ultimate sanction above and beyond our wits' end is part of the essence of our human nature,
an ultimate yes or no hangs above our heads, there and not-
there. If there is a hostile force in all this, it is indifference, the
sealing up of the heart. For after all, God so mysteriously

extends his hand over Cain's head against the vengeance of the world—even to this first murderer there is the mercy of creation. In his terrible way Cain too has served; he has filled out the definition of the real nature of man.

Genesis, the book, is a poem, a poem about a world already teeming with people whom the poet has abstracted, whose essences he has drawn out and composed into a separated archetypical family. The process is hardly different in principle from the way Hamlet and Macbeth are made into archetypes of particular human dilemmas.

So much for the morals of the piece; there is of course the theory that the story depicts the rancher-farmer conflict and is perhaps a warning to the population to cool down what may have been a common source of violence. The key to this interpretation is possibly God's not quite (to Cain) satisfactory assurance that he loves all equally despite the inequality of their rewards at his hands. I wonder if this angle is not reinforced by what happens after Cain is exiled.

He not only gets married but builds Enoch, a city named after his first son. And Enoch begets four children, one of whom takes two wives, and the descendants of these are all, oddly enough, described by their techniques and occupations. One is "the father of such as have cattle"; another, the progenitor of organists and harpists; another is an instructor of brass and iron workers; and finally, and most mysterious of all, there is the declaration of one, Lamech, who tells his wives that he has wounded one man and killed another.

Now God had promised a sevenfold revenge on anyone harming Cain; but "If Cain shall be avenged sevenfold, truly Lamech [shall be avenged] seventy and sevenfold." I don't understand the point being made here, unless the famous Mark of Cain flows through the blood of all his descendants now and forever. And this must mean that we are to withhold our vengeful feelings against murderers, for in them too, farfetched as it often seems,

there is God's love and a potential penitential witness to it—bad
news, it would seem, for death-penalty advocates.

The greatness of the Genesis poem lies in its infinite sugges-
tiveness. It is full of thisness and thatness, and very little why-
ness, and so it tends to keep its reader awake and perhaps a
little more alive.

Like other authors I am not a complete stranger to misunderstanding of my work, especially by the literal-minded.
There was a famous *New Yorker* cartoon in which a man
emerges from the theater where *Death of a Salesman* was playing, saying to his companion, "I've always said that New England territory was no damned good." And in China, where I
directed the play in the Chinese language, an American TV in-
terviewer asked a young man coming out of a performance
what he thought of the play. "Oh, it's very a true play; Willy
Loman is absolutely correct. Everybody wants to be number
one man! That Biff, his son—he's the problem." And indeed,
after nearly half a century of leveling Willy's paeans of praise
to victorious competitiveness must have seemed like the sun
breaking through the mists. This is the same play, of course,
that, when it first came out, was called by one commentator a
"time bomb under Capitalism." I thought so too at the time—
at least of Capitalism's well-known brutalities—but half a century later on the other side of the world the same play became
the voice of personal liberation and implicitly of the virtues of
accumulation of wealth. Go figure.

In any case, God extending a hand over the killer Lamech
seventy-seven times more protectively than even he did over
the head of Cain, the world's first fratricide, must mean something important—if one only knew the context. But I suppose
the texts we understand completely are the ones we are inclined
to forget completely. In short, our misunderstanding with life
and the world and our attempts to clear it up must, if the Bible
is to be at all believed, be a tension that is preserved forever.

The Story
of Abel

Michael Dorris

I had the story all wrong. In
the watered-down morality tale of my grade school Bible Stories book, Abel was simply good and Cain was bad—that easy.
The brothers got equal billing, were costars of their true-life
drama, and there was no doubt which one I was supposed to
emulate. Later, as an altar boy, every time toward the end of the
Mass that I recited *Agnus Dei*, Lamb of God, I thought sympa-
thetically of that ill-fated shepherd, whose only crime was
innocence.

Upon rereading Genesis now, however, I have to conclude
that Abel was little more than a plot device—his existence
and then his death the trigger for more important action. If
Abel didn't exist, as the old saying goes, God would have had
to invent him—which, of course, is precisely what God did.
Cain is the character who rivets our interest. As a writer, I
know that the most facile solution to a complex literary
problem is simply to bump off the protagonist. The challenge
is to let him live, to observe and chronicle the workings out
of consequences. Abel doesn't get a line of dialogue or a

flicker of authorial observation. He picks a sheep that pleases God, and later, when Cain seems about to confront him ("Cain said to his brother Abel . . . ") all that follows is a cryptic ellipsis, as if the words don't much matter in the greater scheme of things.

The episode is related in concise, straightforward prose, as fascinating for what it omits as for what it includes. Adam and Eve have two sons; the elder, Cain, becomes a farmer, and the younger, Abel, a shepherd. When the time comes for them to honor the Lord, Cain apparently just snatches up any old crop—no presentation, no State Fair blue-ribbon quality—but Abel offers the pick of his lambs. Guess who gets praised? Guess whose feelings are hurt? Guess what happens next?

This early on in the Torah virtually everything human is a "first." First children. First relative value of property. First sibling rivalry. First murder. First talking back. Second fall from grace—like father, like son. The apple didn't fall far from the tree.

But here's an odd detail: after Cain slays Abel, is he confronted by his (and Abel's) parents? No, they have disappeared. The fratricide is a crime that must be confessed to and judged by no less than God Himself, and He is not amused. Cain, attempting evasion when God asks what became of Abel, spontaneously blurts the line he's been saddled with ever since: "Am I my brother's keeper?" Talk about giving God an opening! But here's another odd detail: God doesn't reply. The question is left hanging, a plumb line right through history.

God's silence echoes. Was Cain's inquiry sarcastic and devious, as it has often been read? Or was it serious? Abel certainly wasn't Cain's keeper—he didn't advise his brother to offer the premium produce, didn't defend Cain's gift when God turned up His divine nose at it. Plus, there's no indication that Seth, the final child of Adam and Eve, was much of a keeper to Cain.

John Donne argues that "no man is an island," and yet that's
exactly what Cain turned out to be: alone and cut off. Unkept.

The stories one absorbs as a child tend to be accepted whole
and uncritically. Without the benefit of experience to make us
leery, we swallow and avow everything from Santa Claus to the
half-baked sexual mores of playgrounds and locker rooms. We
dwell in a world of absolute orthodoxy—a belief system so
solid that it's easily shattered by the ping mallet of a single dis-
senting realization. Just as the organic technologies of some
tribal peoples can't help but be ecologically pure—if you don't
make anything that lasts, you can't pollute your surroundings—acquired knowledge based solely on faith freely tolerates
paradox and seeming irrationality. But once the plastic of
doubt, the tin can of skepticism, the indestructible Styrofoam
of conflicting intuition intrudes—once, in other words, we eat
of the Tree of Knowledge of Good and Evil—the landscape becomes increasingly, cumulatively cluttered. To return to a pristine environment requires an act infinitely more difficult than
blind trust; it takes will, and sometimes the will to intention-
ally close our eyes on what we see before us.

The battle between wish and logic, between what we want to
be true and what seems to be the case, is ongoing, the balance
tipping first this way and then that as we navigate down the
complicated paths toward maturity and understanding. In my
own case, an instant of decision—to be hopeful or to be
smart—arose in my early twenties when, after almost a year of
application and expectation, I was offered the opportunity,
though I had never been married, to legally adopt a child. I remember very clearly the afternoon when I sat before a social

worker's desk in Littleton, New Hampshire. The man, having just told me of the availability of a three-year-old Lakota boy, opened a manila file and read a long list of statistics: test scores, doctor's opinions, medical analyses. The gist of the information was that the child in question had severe disabilities, both physical and in the area of learning potential. He had been born premature to an alcoholic and abusive mother. He was small for his age, had almost no vocabulary, had not been toilet trained, had been in and out of the hospital with chronic pneumonia.

I heard only one thing: I had a son.

"What's his name?" I asked.

"He's had several different nicknames in various placements. Though it's unusual, I think in this instance, old as he is, you could probably choose to call him anything you like, should you decide to proceed."

I opened my mind, and there, like a time capsule that had waited for the most appropriate moment, was the symbol—because that's what names are, after all—that for me conveyed purity of soul, goodness, the perfection of creation: Abel. I later learned that in Hebrew, Abel means breath.

And, a few weeks later, Abel it was. And, for everyone who encountered him in those early days, he was the embodiment of pre-concupiscence: trusting, loving, thrilled, easily comforted, finding immense joy in every kiss and touch and friendly gesture. Beautiful though painfully thin, Abel was, in an almost four-year-old body, a baby who had just discovered how to smile—and couldn't do enough of it. He was a person who often inspired the use of the term "angel," a boy whose exhilaration, whose unself-conscious fling of himself at life, made the parents of his contemporaries regard their own comparatively sophisticated offspring with melancholy nostalgia. Abel, the "Abel" of my impressionistic memory, was the ideal appellation, the dream I hadn't realized I had dreamt embodied.

And then he grew up, or rather, he didn't. If the world—or perhaps, if only I—had allowed him, tolerated the perpetuation of his frozen moment of development, let him exist in a timeless state, Abel, I think, would not have changed. He would have remained forever that carefree spirit, that exuberant heart, that blissful bright balloon that floated above ordinary notions of "progress."

But no stasis is permitted in the inexorable flux of time. The lamb can't stay a lamb. When Abel didn't keep up with his peers, when he didn't learn to count or read or make judgments on the proper schedule, he was shunned, labeled, ridiculed, or, worse, ignored. Part of his underlying deficiency—the whole syndrome that apparently was the result of his prenatal exposure to alcohol—was lack of understanding, and he didn't "get" why people's behavior toward him altered. By ten, his charm no longer charmed. By twelve, his hugs were no longer reciprocated with unrestrained affection. By fifteen, he was expected to comprehend—and restrain—far more about his sexuality than he did.

Naturally, if only in reaction to the rejection he experienced, Abel developed a darker side. He began to seek the solitude of his own company, to grow unresponsive. He ignored complex instructions, was oblivious to the dictates of clocks and money, abjured well-meaning advice. Before my eyes, invincible to any intervention my family or I might attempt, Abel turned from a sunny child into the kind of adult whose disturbed demeanor causes strangers to cross the street.

———————

God's anger at Cain over Abel's murder was terrifying. "You shall be more cursed than the ground, which opened its mouth to receive your brother's blood from your hand. If you till the soil," God said to this first agriculturist, "it shall no longer yield its strength to you. You shall become a ceaseless wanderer on the earth." Later, recanting slightly when Cain replies, "'My punishment is too great to bear! Since you have banished me this day from the soil, and I must avoid Your presence and become a restless wanderer on earth—anyone who meets me may kill me!' the Lord said to him, 'I promise, if anyone kills Cain, sevenfold vengeance shall be taken on him.' And the Lord put a mark on Cain, lest anyone who met him should kill him. Cain left the presence of the Lord and settled in the land of Nod, east of Eden."

Genesis gets demographically complicated at this point. Suddenly there is a wife for Cain to marry, a population of a city, Enoch, for him to found, and whole tent-dwelling, lyre- and pipe-playing generations to follow. It's as though the author of the story collapses history, fast-forwards creation into a full-blown universe to emphasize the epic nature of the tale. There's no drama, no suspense when the landscape gets inhabited one person at a time—that's just the prologue. Accordingly, as the true line of Adam proceeds via Seth—and Cain and his descendants disappear from center stage—we're in the thick of action-adventure, grand-scale conflict. If this were a film, the segue would be from *My Dinner with André* to Cecil B. DeMille in Panavision.

Brief as it is, the story of Cain and Abel lends itself to many types of interpretation. Its closest analogue in Sumerian folklore repeats the basic agriculture/pastoral dichotomy and also ends with the founding of a city. Viewed from a wider perspective, tales about siblings, often good and evil twins, abound in hundreds of cultural traditions—a way, perhaps, of accounting for humanity's persistent dual and dueling impulses. It is also a saga of the disappointing son who himself is disappointed—when God "paid no heed" to Cain's offering, "Cain was much distressed and his face fell"—with disastrous results.

The archetypical father-and-son struggle inherent in the tale forms the basis for Bruce Springsteen's powerful ballad, "Adam Raised a Cain," in which father and son are described as "prisoners of love" and doomed to intergenerational conflict.

Some ancient biblical commentators, such as Rabbi Shimon bar Yochai (quoted by W. Gunther Plaut in *The Torah: A Modern Commentary*), go so far as to interpret that the implication behind Cain's defiant and defensive rejoinder to the Lord is profoundly far-reaching.

> When God asked Cain 'Where is your brother Abel?' Cain answered 'Am *I* my brother's keeper? You are God. You have created man. It is Your task to watch him, not mine. If I ought not to have done what I did, you could have prevented me from doing it.' Thus Cain makes God responsible or at least co-responsible for his own actions. (p. 47)

For what precisely, though, is Cain marked? Is his major crime fratricide or defiance, a lack of generosity or a failure to appreciate God's ultimate, if arbitrary, power? In the universe of His exclusive devising, God does not have to answer for His actions to Cain or to any other human, does not have to play fair—just ask the Canaanites. Cain, like his parents before him, failed to appreciate humanity's ultimate vulnerability, and for that they paid a high price. It's not until Job that a biblical character seems truly to comprehend how the system works and therefore passes the grueling test.

For me personally, the story originally seemed about accident and fate—subjectively sometimes beneficent, other times immeasurably cruel. If Cain had selected a better vegetable to sacrifice, if God had been more even-handed in His praise, if Cain had merely punched Abel in the nose, if my Abel's mother had consumed less ethanol during her pregnancy, how differently the future might have unfolded. One thing leads to another, and another, and another, and only God gets second chances. The rest of us, like Cain in his tragic as opposed to his jealous mode, simply exist, as Springsteen says, "from the dark heart of a dream," permanently marked, wandering helpless in our private wilderness.

There are no bargains, no guarantees. My son lacked the ability to think abstractly, to anticipate, to forecast consequences, and so, like his namesake, he lived his brief life in a series of compliant acceptances. Joy and sorrow came equally as surprises to him, bolts from the blue. He bore no grudges for he imagined no justice. He followed basic rules and would never have had the initiative to leave the garden, never have taken umbrage at another's elevation, never have been too curious to obey, never questioned his fate. There are moments when I think he was fortunate not to have grasped what he was missing. But I wouldn't trade places with him. To have a sense of good and evil does not by a long shot grant control or peace, but it yields the next best thing: like Cain at his best, we know enough to be angry.

The Story
of Cain

Ron Hansen

Rob and I were Boy Scouts
in Omaha, Nebraska. And it was time to vote for patrol leader,
the highest-ranking officer in Troop Sixteen. We may have
been twelve then. We were still called The Twins. I have forgotten the formalities of the voting, only that it was held in secret,
and the tallying behind closed doors took far longer than it
should have. I have forgotten even who won an election that
seemed hugely important to me then. What I recall is that a
boy other than me was chosen, and I was shocked. Seeing my
face, a friend who'd been in on the tally confided that I had in
fact won the election, but the scoutmaster thought it would
hurt my brother's feelings if I was favored over him.

Walking home with Rob that night I fumed for a few blocks
and then shouted in fury, "It's always going to be this way!
You're always going to hold me back!"

Rob, I remember, looked stricken.

Rob is always Abel in my memories. I am always Cain.

Even as far back as the age of one it was that way. One afternoon Rob was put in his crib and me in mine, and my mother

tried to tiptoe to the door. But I must have been hungry for affection or some further sign of my uniqueness, for as Rob fell asleep and Mom tried to tiptoe to the door, I got up on my knees and held onto the crib slats and shook my head from side to side, saying, "No, no, no, no!" And she thought that so charmingly honest a need that she held me for a few minutes more.

Envy and rivalry. We were paging through magazines on one of those hot and endless August afternoons of childhood when Rob got the notion to try to imitate a photograph of the glamorous, silken spread of Skippy peanut butter on a pristine slice of white bread. I heard him working in the kitchen for too many minutes, and then he proudly strolled back with his honed and sculpted peanut butter creation in his hand. "Look," he said, "it's perfect!"

And it was. Even art of a kind. But, alas, the temptation was just too strong. I whacked the backside of his hand so hard that the peanut butter swocked into his face. Rob was, one could say, dismayed.

"You know, it's funny," my brother said, when I read these pages to him, "but in *my* memories you're always Cain, too."

The feel is that of a fairy tale. The firstborn of the first man and woman was a son, Kayin; and he was followed by another son, Hevel. Kayin grew up to be a farmer, while Hevel herded sheep, and it was their habit at harvest time to offer a sacrifice to God of the first fruits of the fields and the firstlings of the flock, for it was God whose gifts they were. But Kayin grew hard of heart and put on the high altar only the fruits and grains that had fallen on the ground. Was God blind that he couldn't tell the difference? God found fault with Kayin, but favored Hevel, and Kayin fought with his brother over that, and he killed him.

Then God asked Kayin, though he knew, where his brother was,
and Kayin tried to pretend he had no idea. And God's wrath
was great, for he'd heard Kayin's brother's blood crying out
from the reddened ground, and God damned Kayin for his
murder, and damned his tilling of the soil, forcing him to wander the earth, far from the face of God.

Chapter 4:1–16 of the book of Genesis follows up the fall from
paradise with an analogical tale in which a second generation
is offered the choice of obedience or estrangement, of heeding
God's warnings or facing death. With the Cain and Abel narrative we get the first mention of sin and the first statement of
the important themes of family conflict and competition that
permeate this book of begettings. If the story was adapted, as
some propose, from an older folktale about the hostilities
among shepherds and farmers, the correspondence between
source and finished text is no doubt as far distant as that between Holinshed's *Chronicles* and Shakespeare's *Macbeth*. For
the raw power and wisdom and psychological complexity in
this fable are wholly lacking in other ancient texts, where the
focus was on a pantheon of glamorous gods, and flesh-and-
blood humanity was thought to be an unworthy subject for
writerly expression. In fact, reading contemporaneous texts
only heightens the awe one feels for the economy, sophistica-
tion, and primal force of this book of genius.

We feel the far-ranging influence of Cain and Abel throughout the Hebrew Bible; in the Gospel narratives of Jesus, the
good shepherd, and Judas, his betrayer; and further on in the
old English Mystery plays that were performed on high holy
days such as Whitsuntide or the feast of Corpus Christi. The
fall from paradise was, of course, a popular theme among the
slogging farmers and trade unionists who wanted particular

someones to blame for their hard lot. And no one was more villainous than Cayn, or Cayme, a rough and raffish peasant much like themselves, but avaricious and arrogant, too, like the lords and high-and-mighties in the cities. Often Cain withheld his finest produce out of spite for his misfortunes, offering God the fallen corn on the ground on the principle that if Cain and his family were forced to eat that, it ought to be good enough for His Highness. Abel fulfilled the function of village priest in the Mysteries, worshiping and thanking God with an offering of the finest of his flock. While Cain is hot-tempered, insolent, and sullen, Abel is all piety and rectitude, too good to be true, even a bit of a simp; a hand raised against him seems oddly fitting, and there must have been more than a few in the audiences who felt a forbidden pleasure at seeing him laid out.

Lord Byron interestingly altered the old tradition with *Cain,* an ill-received psychological drama in which the first murderer is an aspiring and proud intellectual whose high estimate of himself is sundered when, on a journey into space and the past, Lucifer offers him an illustration of his own paltriness in comparison with infinite things. Abased, brooding, and despondent, Cain finds in Abel's bloody sacrifice a shame to creation, and in heedless fury at a Creator who has burdened humanity with frailties and inadequacies, Cain strikes down his brother with an iron. His blood flowing into the ground, Abel has time for one last prayer: that his own soul be received into Heaven and that Cain be forgiven "for he knew not what he did." Looking about him, as though jolted from a sleep, Cain asks, "Where am I? Alone! Where's Abel? Where Cain? Can it be that I am he? My brother, awake! Why liest thou so on the green earth? 'Tis not the hour of slumber." Cain's crime is not one of villainy or malice, but of rebellion and mischance, and when he finds out what he's done, he's filled with remorse. We do not suffer with him, however. We can do little more than sigh.

Each of these later renditions is hobbled by the character of Abel. The first victim of the first murder is perhaps a man to pity, but we feel no ache at his loss. Abel slides off the page like a bookmark, a symbol of what we ought to be, a fine abstraction, like righteousness, that we agree our friends should pursue with far greater diligence. We have learned, since the Book of Genesis, that a good plot requires worthy opponents, a fitting antagonist to the protagonist, such as Peter Shaffer offers us in *Amadeus*.

Here Cain is Antonio Salieri, an Italian composer in the Viennese court and a former teacher of Ludwig van Beethoven, who has discovered, after forty-one operas, a requiem mass, and a surfeit of sacred music, that his work is dull and mediocre, wholly lacking in passion. The focus of his education is Wolfgang Amadeus Mozart, for Salieri hears him play on the piano his *Serenade for 13 Wind Instruments* and is shaken by the absolute beauty of the piece. At their next meeting, when Salieri welcomes Herr Mozart to the Viennese court with his own rather pedestrian march, Mozart is fascinated by the wrong turns Salieri's composition took and with a few effortless flourishes transforms it into a masterpiece. And Salieri finds himself thinking of murder, not out of hatred for Mozart, but for God, who unfairly has lavished such talent and virtuosity on a conceited, spiteful, infantile "creature" while withholding it from him.

My own pale variation on the fable of Cain and his brother was played out in my historical novel *The Assassination of Jesse James by the Coward Robert Ford*. I found in my research that Bob Ford had been obsessed by the James gang ever since he was a boy, frequently imagining himself as one of them, but also thinking of the fame he would garner if he were to capture one of the outlaws. His chance came when he and his brother Charley insinuated themselves as friends of Jesse during his and his brother Frank's final train robbery, in Blue Cut, Missouri.

The James gang fell apart after that hold-up, as one man after the next was either killed or jailed. Ever watchful, even paranoid, Jesse James for some reason failed to suspect that Bob Ford was conspiring with the government to arrest or assassinate him. But perhaps Jesse intended to kill the Ford brothers himself when he invited them to the house on a hill in St. Joseph, Missouri, where he was hiding with his wife and two children under the alias of Thomas Howard. Quite possibly he was simply mistaken about the Ford brothers' seeming friendship, and what Jesse interpreted as hero worship and flattery and imitation were in fact the scheming and dissembling of petty thieves. Bob Ford finally did not so much want to be *like* Jesse James, as he thought in his youth, but wanted rather to *be* him. The factual human being was in the way of his own fabulous dreams of himself. And so he betrayed his friend by firing his gun into the back of his head as Jesse frittered about in his house one April morning in a kind of cat-and-mouse game. Hearing the gunfire, Zerelda James ran out of the kitchen and fell on her knees by her husband, who was lying slain on the floor. She looked up at the Ford brothers and asked Bob, much as God asked Cain, "What have you done?" And, like Cain, Bob tried to shirk culpability for his crime, saying the gun went off accidentally.

Bob was treated as a hero for a short time after the shooting, but was given only a portion of the financial reward he sought and was forced to find an income through theatrical reenactments of his crime. Each night, in far-away towns, his brother Charley would have a blank fired at his head as he portrayed the famous killer who was killed. Each night Bob Ford would tell the audience, without shame or remorse, just how he did what he did. As time went on, Charley could not handle the hatred they increasingly felt from the crowds, and within a few years he committed suicide. But Bob haughtily continued, like

Cain a fugitive and vagabond on the earth, until he fetched up in Creede, Colorado, where he owned a tavern and where one night he was killed by a shotgun blast from a drunken man named Ed O'Kelly who claimed he did it to avenge his fallen idol. Blood will have blood.

In the King James Version of the Bible, the Lord warns Cain, "If thou doest well, shalt thou not be accepted? and if thou doest not well, sin lieth at the door. And unto thee shall be his desire, and thou shalt rule over him." And in the next sentence, "it came to pass, when they were in the field, that Cain rose up against Abel his brother, and slew him."

I find it a chilling story, even in its fleeting telling, even with so much left out. We so often find ourselves ruled by sin that the fate of Cain seems not far off at all. I have, for example, one more memory. Rob and I were teenagers, and in the kitchen one night. He washed the dishes; I dried them. We weren't arguing. But as we goofed off I flipped the dish towel over his head and astonished him by roughly tightening it at his neck and holding it taut. Was there hostility in it? I felt no emotion, only a kind of fierce energy and fascination— *Look what I can do.* And then he fell to his knees and onto his back. His face was white as I knelt over him. Life seemed to be leaking onto the floor. Was murder that easy? Right then I was thinking I was going to be in big trouble if our folks found out I'd killed him. You just don't do that sort of thing. Slapping his cold cheeks like they do in movies, and hushing my voice in order to keep my heinous crime hidden for a little longer, I whispered, "Wake up! Please, Rob! Please don't die!"

Rob opened his eyes in bland surprise and sheepishly looked at me. "What happened?"

With huge relief I sat back on my heels and got into a change of character. "You fainted," I told him, and helped him to his feet. We finished washing the dishes in silence, as if nothing had happened, and I heard the television on in the living room, and the shrieks of a sitcom audience, and the soft laughter of my parents.

The Story
of Noach

David Mamet

Let us suppose, as Freud
suggests, that there is the *manifest* dream, the dream we remember; and there is the *latent* dream—the dream the manifest dream is constructed to obscure, the dream we would
rather forget, which is too powerful, too upsetting, too unset-
tling. The memory/dream of infant sacrifice becomes cleansed
into the Binding of Isaac; the memory of infanticide becomes
Moses's shattering of the tablets.

The second, or prettier, dream in the Noach story is the
Tower of Babel.

Human beings, the story informs us, when they associate
into large groups, inevitably set about mischief; they are sus-
ceptible to outward and inward exhortations to idolatry, that
is, to self-worship. They wrongly reason or intuit that if one
person is powerful, the group must be geometrically more
powerful of arm, reason, intellect—that given a large enough
group, nothing is impossible. We see such an error in the
Tower of Babel, and in its most modern rendition, the Information Superhighway, and, in fact, in all of human history in

between. Banding together into large groups leads to idolatry, folly, and destruction. Manifest Destiny, the Monroe Doctrine, the Gulf of Tonkin Resolution, the House Un-American Activities Committee—in these we can see, from a remove, the very exuberance engendered by solidarity as a diagnostic tool of arrogance and the inevitable cruelty to which it leads. "America First," the "Horst Wessel Lied," "Desert Storm," such self-assured, fervent communal activity allows us to submerge ourselves and our conscience, to lay down the burden of uncertainty, to disregard the ambiguous and the difficult. We can and do characterize this happiness as "being made whole," but the Torah tells us we should be warned that "being made whole" by a sense of our own power is not a healthy state; it is idolatry and leads directly to grief.

Our American wonder at having saved the world in 1945 and our efforts to prolong that feeling led to Vietnam, to Korea, to Desert Storm, to a country debased and impoverished by the defense establishment, and the necessity of a constant Evil Oppressor.

"Do not band together into Large groups, you will do Evil." This is the *manifest* dream; it is clear, it is logical, it is, in effect, a straightforward morality tale: "In situation A do not act as these characters do, or, as you see, unfortunate results will ensue."

That is the Tower of Babel, but the Tower story is the manifest, the scrambled, the encrypted/cleansed version of a previous, *latent* dream, which it attempts to master through repetition. And the latent dream is not a cautionary tale, it is a straight-out horror. "You have been sinning, and I, HaShem, repent me of having made the World, and I will destroy it. And the waters prevailed, and all the high mountains that were under the heavens were covered, and all HaShem had made was obliterated."

In fact, the waters rose to fifteen cubits *above* the high mountains, "And all in whose nostrils was the breath of life, of all that were on dry land, died."

In the first dream, the latent dream, the Flood, HaShem saw that the wickedness of man was very great, and that all imagination and every thought of his heart was only evil continually. *Rah Rah Col HaYom.* No repentance is possible, all are destroyed, as all are evil. But Noach, we are told, found grace in the eyes of the Lord.

But Freud said that just as the manifest hides the latent dream, so the latent dream conceals a primal, infantile trauma. And we might suggest that the height of the waters—fifteen cubits *over* the mountains—indicates that the flood deals with a *further* submerged memory: that the waters rise not only sufficient to obliterate all life, but to a height sufficient to make any attempt at retrospection bootless. The Land (the Old Life) cannot even be discerned (remembered). Why?

I believe the story is about the wish to kill—that the world-destruction dream, "Every thing was killed in the flood," hides the fury-rage-anger of the primitive-infantile idea: I wish to Destroy the World, I have been angered and wish to kill not only those who anger me, but *everyone.* My anger (so reasons the infant mind) is all-powerful as *I* am all-powerful, I do not need an excuse, I, myself, am the occasion . . . what could be better than to kill?

"And it came to pass, when men began to multiply on the face of the Earth, and daughters were born to them, that the sons of God saw the daughters of men, that they were fair, and they took themselves wives of all whom they chose and there were giants in the Earth." Who were these giants? The parents. Why is the writer wroth? He/she wants to be the sole object of the giants' attention and cannot compete with the attraction of adult sexuality, and so wants the Earth to be destroyed.

So the double-encrypted wish-dream in the Noach story is
the memory of the desire to renounce/forget murder. And,
once again, we have the psychological cauldron of the Second
Son who inverts his hatred of the elder brother (and perhaps
his guilt at survival of ritual sacrifice), and projects the guilt as
the desire of the older brother to kill *him*. What must the child
feel, what must the infant feel, what must the race feel, that
grew up in a culture practicing infant sacrifice? The unformed
mind must see its wildest and most cherished fantasies enacted
and endorsed, and devoted itself to the creation of an idol that
would require and endorse such actions and so relieve the individual of guilt: for example, Baal, Godless Communism,
Peace in Our Time, The American Way, The Revolution. . . .

That one cannot have what one wants—world dominion,
infallibility, boundless wealth—that one *should* not have what
one wants, that idolatry is a destructive, infantile state the tro-
pism toward which must be superseded, is the message of
Noach. The message of the Torah is that though we conquer
our lower nature once, and at the beginning, and again and
again, it will reassert itself, for that's what it is to be human.
The clean and the unclean animals will be on the ark, the sons
of Noach will begin to build the tower at the conclusion of the
Begats, and though the world be submerged and the mountains be covered to the depth of fifteen cubits, the Torah time
and again and continually informs us that there is a story beneath the story and that the very fact of its encryption should
compel our interest and study.

The Story of the
Tower of Babel

David Shapiro

I *feel more and more that
we must not judge of God from this world, it's just a study
that didn't come off. What do you do with a study that has
gone wrong? . . . It's only a master who can make such a
blunder. . . .*

Van Gogh, Letters

*Unless the Lord builds the house,
its builders labor in vain. . . .*

Psalm 127

We do not customarily pray in the direction of the Tower of
Babel. It is, perhaps, more of a tradition among secularists,
modernists, and Spinozists like myself. We find ourselves praying to what we see: the artist Brueghel and his bright painterly
burrow; and we pray in our personal noncollective way in the
direction of the starry chaos of Proust and Kafka's inner and
outer burrow. We pray and don't pray; we find it impossible to
pray; we take our place carrying the holes of the philosophers

and poets. The hole is the tradition. Otherwise, some pray to
Rimbaud and give up in the great tradition of personal silence.

Emmanuel Levinas, the contemporary French Jewish
philosopher, rebukes us and suggests that like Spinoza, we may
simply not have had good enough Hebrew teachers. Otherwise, we might more fully partake of his parable in which two
arks are carried. In one a man lies who has accomplished the
law contained inside the other. But for us, too often, the arks
have become coffins. So then, at least, we acknowledge the
power of the stories, and if not the whole narrative, the jokes,
and if not the jokes the endless dispute, and if not the dispute,
the horrible artfulness of those who would destroy us and the
endlessness of our dispute. After all, the dispute is our Tower.
"A strong tower against the enemy."

In the midst of Fritz Lang's dazzling and infantile film classic, *Metropolis,* lies an uncanny tower within a tower and a
midrash, or rabbinical commentary, from the purist Maria.
She recounts to her protofascist audience the Babel story, in
which the elite planners grind into dust such lumpen who construct it. She, the simple-minded Mediator of this film beloved
of Hitler, concludes that the story demands a mediation between architectural mind and the vascular hand of the herd
that builds. After the pyramids, a new Passover! The more
grisly element of *Metropolis* remains within its film-noir mists:
a vision of the shocking city as Moloch into which we are
poured like so much nutritious cement. And Lang's response
to Hitler resonates ironically. Invited to head the German film
industry, the artist fled in the night with visions of an unmedi-
ated Babel. Dispersal, centripetal flower, kept him alive for the
classic *Contempt* and other film-making integrities.

Isn't dispersal worse than death, and isn't such a scattering
better than death? All the commentaries agree to disagree. The
story must be placed next to Noah's destroyed contemporaries.
Noah's generation was butchered in a stormy allegory for its

disunity in murderous internecine corruption. Meanwhile,
the Babel Tower was built with urbane or imperial unity. A
unity that was only punishable by multiplicity, of course. Even
the modern Hebrew poet Bialik speaks of the two essential
movements of the Jewish people as dispersal and homecom-
ing. And further, the Babel story speaks of the essential con-
centrate of "civilization" as either a profound mistake or
monstrous excess. A Blakean reading, for instance, will permit the Tower always to be more interesting than the sin of
building it. After the covenant, we hardly expect a rainbow behind this Ziggurat, but we are compelled to see the story as a
uniquely horrifying addendum to the Rainbow. A covenant
of peace with man is immediately followed by a story of immense penology. The Tower appeals as an invasive prong with
the requisite sense of an Antagonist. If the Tower is not built
to last, it is at the least scaled with seven Assyrian rungs to
Paradise. Mies Van der Rohe, the modern architect par excel-
lence, would have approved.

When I was a boy of ten or so, my uncle gave me a book on
modern art that included an illustration of Mies's Glass Tower
project. The transparent splendor of this futuristic folly struck
me, and his abstractions became my obsession, yielding an
image of eternity. It is always suggestive to remember the paradox that architecture is a private, tragic, and fragile art. Books
may last longer than buildings, and Shelley's "Ozymandias" is
part of the correct commentary on the hubris of place and the
Jewish denunciation of such a spectral architecture. Babel hor-
rifies with the connotations of ceaseless metropolitan work and
its naked assertion that architecture may dominate time. The
Babel fable italicizes the fragility of all human construction, as if
it were all an Assyrian astrology. The majesty of the Babel story
is its naked condensation. It is a teaching story, and the rabbis
have understandably loved it, as in the great commentary that a
lost brick would cause more tears in Babel than a fallen worker.

Is it language that rises or falls here? Architecture is married to poetry in our story, and no commentator can escape this sacred synthesis. The rise of the city of arrogance is the end of a language without puns. The Hebrew language should have been the sufficient blueprint of a perfect world. The apple of language rots upon touch, and disintegrates at the foot of the Tower. The perfect language is murdered by multiplicity. Here, Jewish wisdom is most divided. On the one hand, the commentaries teach us that the scattering is good and brings Jewish wisdom into the many worlds of history. But it is also the world of babble indeed, the multiple shifting perspectives of an exile in horror and falsity. Architecture rises as the somber specter of such fallen man, fallen tongues, and the exile of mistranslating. It is for this reason that a critic like George Steiner emphasized in lectures I heard in Cambridge in the late 1960s that the true moderns were bilingual and exiled essentially to that condition of multiplicity. We live in the condition of the collage at the end of the Wasteland, and only the macaronic cadenzas of the Wake bring us the proper sense of the inner and outer exile of our lives. The happiest view is that such multiplicity, like autumn coloration, is not functional but a happy scandal of abundance. God scatters us into his abundance, on a wave of language. Here, I think of Roman Jakobson, of whom it was said that he shouted for help, when struck by a car, in forty-seven languages. Poetry may be this cry for help in forty-seven languages. The Flood of languages produces an odd covenant. We may find, with Steiner, that language "after Babel" will henceforth be the master of the nations.

———————

Ricky Small, my best pal, and I would meet in 1959 with Tzionah Ben Tzvi in my house in Newark to have tutorials for our Bar Mitzvahs. I was going to a Hebrew school, Bet Yeled, that emphasized a lot of singing of Zionist songs and "Hebrew

as a living language." On violin I was learning the Hebrew
Melody by Achron with the cadenza by Auer for a concert after
the Bar Mitzvah, to compensate for my lack of a voice. Achron
had known my grandfather, and it was reported also that the
jazzy accompaniment to the Melody was influenced by their
taste for Harlem forays.

My grandfather, one of the golden Chazzanim (cantors),
had died praying in 1954 at the local Young Israel. I brooded
and was told this was the best death. A few years ago, research-
ing his career and finding a scrapbook given to him after a
decade in South Africa, I found an interview with him under
the headline: "I Want to Die Singing." I was always hypnotized
by his voice, at table or on the old 78s, a sweet tenor with a col-
oratura falsetto. The doctors, I was told, had warned against
such embellishment: it could darken the voice. It was a way to
produce the sense of forbidden instruments in a synagogue.

After the story of Noah in Genesis comes the building of the
great cities. The names shock us like a noise, and I hear these
names the way I saw the Assyrian reliefs at the Metropolitan
Museum last year. The Assyrian works were as sophisticated
and severe as a horrible Pop mural, crammed with bleeding
lions. Babylon, Erech, Accad, Calneh. Names that have crum-
bled more times than an obelisk or a late Romantic. Nineveh,
Calah, Babel. The refined and beautiful small writing of the
Assyrians was strangely elegant as any hanging garden beside a
ziggurat—and reproducible in cunning seals. The great cities
in the nude of their names strode past us.

We begin with a dream of sacred unity: God and his people
are one (at least, they speak the same transparent language).
The city emerges from an enormous migration, physical and
spiritual. We are given with naturalistic economy the materialism of their means: "Come, let us make bricks and burn them

hard." It is possible that the Tower was no larger than a department store in today's Manhattan, but the urge was the irresistible conquest of a starry summit. "A tower with its top in the sky." Who can resist the appeal of this structure? There is hardly an interior, just the desolate summit for a Babylonian astronomy. There is nothing wrong with the architect, but collaborative projects like this communal science are intrinsically flawed. Our fable will yield the adventures of history after this astrological assault.

And even God must "come down" to look. There is something grandly theatrical in this descent after the naming of the great cities. Perhaps even the supernal Draughtsman is silently jealous of the little humanist science below with its cognitive invasion of the sky. It is after the time of the intercourse between angels and man. It is a time after the obliteration of Noah's corrupt generation. Now God pronounces, but only to himself or angels, that this rebellion will leave "nothing out of their reach." And so the urbanists have forced the Deity out of his refuge. The Tower has reached those clouds that occluded his Unity.

I was always struck in my youth by the first great and seemingly absurd question—"Where are you?"—asked of Adam in the profanation of his vows. A riddling question in Eden, since the Architect sees every locus in the forest and may pierce every shameful mind. But the Tower of Babel is another epitome of a shamelessness that almost works. The scattering begins with a tidal wave of language. Word and object are divided for the philosophers, and home itself is disseminated into the nations. With this story, we have a kind of parenthesis in the covenant. Does it look forward to the worst in our century? The rabbis have noted that technology and civilization itself are implicated, as the great project occasions a never-ending punishment.

It is hard for us not to look at this as a little fairy tale in the Russian mode of "It was and it was not." Jakobson has said that modernity itself is the palpability that emerges in the division of sign and object in such a space of crushed realism. This fable—part cartoon and part anti-imperial document—is filled economically with a great and concentrated mistrust in palpability. And the scandal is that the Tower is a success. It still exists and is very like Rome or London or New York. Gigantism shouldn't bother us any more than the bewildering smallest brick. We were driven out to become geologists and businessmen, gunrunners and silent, disillusioned carriers of dictionaries. Multiplicity is indeed both our curse and blessing and the true Dark Tower: Time, in which we place our indestructible lack of serenity.

My son Daniel writes his own midrash: "The people were angry at God for making them stop working on their religious spirit the Tower of Babel. Their work was over and their thoughts of seeing God were gone too. It's sad how God didn't want to show himself to the world. He probably thought the world wasn't ready. The Tower of Babel if it was still made would show the world how close mankind got to God." This commentary is not far from certain Talmudic perspectives, and it is also close to the naturalistic echo of Babylonian "gates to God," where a romantic science could have been practiced.

————————

One wants an encyclopedia of the images of tohu bohu—of confusion, chaos—and our best art may be nothing but the illustration of that majestic, essential word. Since my earliest Hebrew classes, after the comic-book Bibles and the childhood vision of God glimpsed in the Atlantic Ocean as a destroyer and a voice, this word has appealed to me as a burden and a dissertation. First chaos, then the world. I have always kept on my desk, next to the red folio and the blue dictionaries, the Bible given to me by my grandmother with the pathos of her inscription that I return to it as to a perfect language. Tohu bohu made its entrance into the French language, but I see it as something more astonishing than formlessness.

To speak, to confuse, to approach a false Paradise: this is the triple pun of our story. The lost original was either a ziggurat for the purposes of worshiping Marduk and the stars, a parable concerning city and language, or a combination of elegy and fable to denounce Empire and its bituminous ashes. The scholars are almost right—Man and God do not speak to each other in these fables. But they do not always understand the triple meaning of this separation: one from the other, ourselves from ourselves, the others from the One. We have lost the words to speak of such lost unities. We are saved only when confounded in a community of exile, and we will enlighten others only by striving to resurrect a truer architecture and an imperfect, more natural poetry: a gate to the unconfused earth.

The Story of Abraham

James Carroll

I thought I knew this story. An old man, cozily retired, is suddenly confronted by one named "Yahweh," who orders him to pack up and leave home. With this conscription from out of nowhere comes a twofold promise—that the old man will be provided with land and descendants. The latter is an especially pointed commitment, since his wife is "barren," and he himself, at "seventy-five," would seem to be past the age of siring children. Nevertheless, he responds without a reported word of hesitation, setting in motion the greatest chain of events the world has known, as well as an infinity of minor events—like my sitting here at this table today.

The old man is Abraham, of course, and his willingness to uproot himself on the strength of Yahweh's word gives the three religions that spring from him one compelling paradigm; gives him claim to the title "father of the faith"; gives pop psychology an image of the trust required to move through the stages of life; and gives risk-averse homilists a perennial way to talk about taking a chance on God. All this, and—to my surprise—it gives a writer like me a new way to think of his work. The story of my own call to writing has changed more than once in my life. Politics of the anti-war era bled into a literary impulse, and for a time aesthetics became the meaning by which I measured faith. Yet in the end, the many stories—religious, political, and literary—all carry the same point, and it is the one I find embedded in these few verses that give us our first Abraham. Uprootedness. Marginality. The permanent departure. The elusive arrival. The endless condition of looking on from outside. I have spent my time trying to find another way to live than this, but I know full well it is the only way to write.

The story of the call of Abraham is given at the beginning of the twelfth chapter of Genesis. What I see now, on a closer and fuller reading, is that this familiar morality tale about risking all in response to Yahweh's promise reaches to only one dimension of what is reported. The story's meaning grows far richer, for example, when seen in the context of what comes immediately before. In chapter 11, God's concern still extends to the entire human scope of His creation. We hear of the tower of Babel and the patriarchs after the Flood, and we recognize the established Genesis motif of creation myth. We are still in the realm of pre-history.

"History" begins when the focus shifts from the universal to the specific, from the era of "once upon a time" to "that time then." At the very end of chapter 11, exactly such a shift begins to occur with the last named post-Flood patriarch, Terah, who "became the father of Abram, Nahor and Haran." With this introduction of "Abram," biblical narrative changes its character entirely, for unlike Noah, Cain, Abel, Eve, or Adam, this partic-

ular man is a human being who exists at a particular time,
even if our archaeology cannot precisely date it, and at a particular place, traces of which abound. The choice he makes at
that juncture of time and place has real-world consequences
that can still be felt in our time and place. The call of Abraham
marks the beginning of human historical consciousness, a direct consequence of the simple statement that God meets
human beings by meeting one human being at one time and at
one place. The God who addresses Himself to Abraham in effect orders him to leave the realm of the purely mythic for "the
land I will show you." Here is the difference between Abraham's God and the gods of Ur or Egypt—He acts not out of
time, but in it; not in the other world, but in this one; not in
"heaven," but in history.

In the stories of Adam and Noah, the deity is named simply
"God," but the one who addresses Himself to Abraham is
named "Yahweh." In this first encounter with Abraham, the
God who will eventually be known as Yahweh of Israel, Father
of Jesus, and Allah of Mohamet reveals Himself, showing us
everything we need to know about Him. The first fact—that He
operates in history, within boundaries of space and time—is
the most important revelation of all. This Creator is invested in
His creation not in general, but in particular. The covenant an-
nounced to the mythical Noah was as elusive as its emblem
rainbow, which seems to touch the earth, but really doesn't. By
contrast, the promise made to Abraham—"It is to your descendants that I will give this land"—offers a set place in which a
named people will live. The seal of this covenant is not a rainbow but the place itself and the people who settle it—beginning
with the physical children of Abraham and Sarah. In the previous chapters of Genesis, God's concern was with "all creation,"
but from now on, it will be with this obscure bridge region between the two high cultures of Egypt and Mesopotamia, and

with a single tribe of wandering sheep merchants who criss-cross the region and then settle down in it.

A second point about the God who shows himself here—this God is *other*. The call of Abraham initiates a relationship of separate beings, one divine, one human. Unlike competing gods then and now, this one makes no promise of a mystical union in which the differences between creature and Creator will be obliterated. When we describe Abraham as the "father of faith," we imply that the religions that come from him are religions of faith, not of union. "Faith" takes for granted the unbridgeable distance between us and God. Indeed, faith sees that distance as the way things are meant to be. Therefore, what to others may seem like alienation seems to Abraham and his descendants like the pre-condition of reciprocity. Because we are not God, never will be, and never hope to be, we can be the friends of God. We can be God's people. Because Abraham's religion is not a religion of mystical union, in other words, it can be a religion of love.

Such relationship, of course, implies not only distance but conflict. The possibility of love presumes the possibility of its opposite. God, in His freedom, initiates. Abraham, in his freedom, responds. But subsequent verses even of this chapter in Genesis—Abraham's lie about Sarah, his offer of Sarah as a bribe to Pharaoh—establish that Abraham's will is not identical with God's. And that, we are clearly meant to see, is the way *this* God wants things to be.

And who is this but a God of history whose interest has moved from the universal to the particular, and a God of freedom who invites a response, but does not coerce it, and whose will is not thwarted even by conflict? The author of these verses has had a true revelation about God, yes. But not only that. The implications of this revelation for religion are, of course, momentous, and have been played out ever since the

call of Abraham in the three Abrahamic faiths. But this revelation reaches not only to the believer's soul but to—our other
theme in this volume—the writer's imagination.

The sacred author speaks to every author here. We recognize
the source of this leap to a new idea about God as being implicit in the form of the story itself. The storytelling author
penetrates the work, literally, at hand; discovers it to be, literally, a sacrament. Indeed, the story is the first sacrament, revealing that what is true of writing is true of God is true of
writing—which surely explains why here begins the religion of
the Word.

For writers, the lessons of all of this are clear. Particularity
and conflict are two pillars of narrative art, and another three
are place, time, and otherness. The law of particularity forces
fiction writers, poets, and dramatists to obsess over details, in-
stances, and concrete images, while treating the experience of
one or two characters as if it matters as much as the sum total
experience of the entire human race. To writers, a moment in
time, properly rendered, is worth all time; a single, vividly
imagined place is worth the cosmos. History is the record of
the causal link between human choice and consequence, and
as the very word implies, history in that sense is the ground of
story itself.

And as there is the law of particularity, there is the law of
polarity. Writers know that without conflict there is no story.
When Coleridge defines the writerly imagination as the seat of
the reconciliation of opposites, he is pointing both to the
writer's method—narrative form presumes movement
through complications—and the writer's subject—how conflict leads to crisis, which leads to resolution. Note that the
writer's aim is not the obliteration of opposites—mystical
union—but their reconciliation—an outcome in which each
polarity has its independent integrity affirmed. Every story

celebrates the recognition that what seemed like contradiction is, in the end, only paradox.

———————————

From the point of view of faith, we see that by coming to Abraham, God comes to all of us; we human beings are the "great nation." From the point of view of the imagination, we see in Abraham's story—exactly because it is not ours—a version of every story, ironically including ours. Either way, the universal is approached only through the particular; the many through the one.

Religiously speaking, we see that God is entirely unlike us, which is why we can have faith in Him. A writer points to the same mystery every time he invents a character of whom no reader ever thought before, yet in whose story the reader finds reverberations of his own experience. Otherness. Conflict. The scandal of particularity. The stuff of faith—and the makings of the writing we love. All of it present in the primordial declaration, "Leave your country, your family and your father's house, for the land I will show you. I will make you a great nation." And all of it present in the large-hearted marvel of a response that this declaration elicited: "So Abram went as Yahweh told him."

The Story
of Lot

Alfred Corn

G*enesis* is the Greek title
(meaning "generation") for the sacred book in Hebrew called
Bereshit after its first word, "in the beginning." Yet the new
name "Generation" is not untrue to the overall import of the
book. Translators of the Greek Septuagint must have been inspired by the Hebrew word *toledot,* which means "generations"
or "begettings," a term appearing over and over again in this
text. Beginnings, engenderings, and genealogies, all of these
compose Genesis's *toledot,* a sacred history covering a period
of, if we take the book's chronologies at face value, some 2,400
years. Genesis begins with God creating all that is—all that is,
that is, apart from the very God who was before creation and
for all time. Creation is itself the first of the *toledot,* an over-
plus or engendering made by Godhead, as we see in 2:4, "These
are the generations [*toledot*] of the heavens and the earth." Like
so many deities of Middle Eastern antiquity, Yahweh (or
YHWH) is a sky god, associated with the heavens. In this understanding, Earth becomes a partner in a continuing creation,
a place where flower and fruit, beasts of the field, and birds of

the air are engendered. And finally, humankind is created, beginning with Adam, from whose side an engendering rib is taken and transformed into Eve, her name in Hebrew meaning "mother of all living," because all generations of humankind proceed from her.

Narrative in *Genesis* begins in a mythic past with Adam and Eve in an innocent garden ("paradise" has the etymological root "garden") and concludes, roughly 1,500 verses later, with the embalmed body of Joseph being laid in a coffin. (His remains do not return to Canaan, as he requested, until Moses takes them there, that delivery recounted in Exodus 13.) Joseph's story is, mythically, in keeping with events confirmed in other historical references to the sojourn of the Hebrews in the land of Egypt. One way to read Genesis is as a transition from myth to protohistory, which involves an "engendering" of history *by* myth (sacred story). At some point in time, Judaic tradition begins to lend the radiance and depth of timeless archetypes to actual events, to incorporate them into written salvation narratives. The last historical event (165 B.C.E.) to be transformed into sacred story is the quasi-miraculous recovery of Jerusalem when the Maccabees defeated Antiochos Epiphanes and shortly after rededicated the Temple that the Seleucid Hellenizer had done everything imaginable to profane. This historical event gradually came to be accepted as a holiday to be celebrated in the religious calendar—and so Chanukkah, the Feast of Dedication, was officially generated. In recent decades, some have proposed that the Shoah also receive a similar consecration. If it does, the People of the Book will thereby only continue a process or practice that began nearly three thousand years ago—the hallowing of the community's life on earth, in historical time. That consecration does not mean that historical time will have as much depth and radiance—or even as much narrative economy—as those ancient, primal stories. The Fall of Adam and Eve may also be understood as a "fall"

from myth into history, which, even if to some degree sacraliz- able, cannot manifest an intrinsic power equal to myth per se.
A sense of that declination must go very deeply into Judaic
consciousness, as can be judged by many indicators. For example, Hebrew writing, unlike later Western languages, moves
from the right to the left. Scribes who wrote the first "in the beginning" of the *Bereshit* scroll moved from the good direction
to the less good for each line of the story, all the way to the end,
with Joseph entombed in Egypt, far from the Promised Land.

Western poetry since Dante has more and more incorporated
the story of the author into the substance of poetry, a process
analogical to the Judaeo-Christian transformation of historical
time into something with more than topical interest. What
Dante and many subsequent poets have done is to turn the
substance of their own lives into a narrative that develops
mythic resonances, at least to the degree that such develop-
ments do not falsify biographical fact. In English poetry, this
approach draws fresh impetus from the Romantics, especially
Wordsworth. In America, the poetry of Whitman and Dickinson
presides over all subsequent efforts to engender the poet's own
story with a mythic dimension. Even when American poetry
turns inward, it is still personal, still narrative, an account of
successive mental states, the psyche's quest backward toward
origins or forward to the Great Good Place. Granted, merely
reciting the events of a life or stages of consciousness in a vainly
glorified CV is never enough to make the quantum leap into a
poetry of mythic strength. Poets attempting that will have to
apprentice themselves and make a study of "monuments of
unageing intellect," otherwise there's no chance of approxi-
mating the primal power of myth.

If you are brought up hearing the Bible read over and over
again, inevitably the narratives you tell in turn about yourself

*Alfred
Corn*

and your community will bear the stamp of those first stories, which become points of reference for so much of experience, during childhood and after. For me and for so many others in the Bible Belt, the book of Genesis was at an early age consecrated in biblical adjectives (like "Edenic"), clichés ("He's as old as Methuselah"), proverbs ("In Adam's Fall we sinned all"), song lyrics ("We Are Climbing Jacob's Ladder"), and universally comprehensible iconography (a dove bearing the olive branch as a sign of peace). Time and expanding knowledge have only brought to my attention more and more examples, high and low, of Genesis's thoroughgoing penetration of Western culture—everything from Milton's *Paradise Lost* to Thomas Mann's *Joseph and His Brothers,* the so-called "sodomy laws" on the books of no small number of the states of the Union, the rainbow flag of the American multicultural left, and the Macintosh Apple computer's logo of an apple with a bite taken out of it. As for my own work, I have not written more than one or two poems based on biblical characters as such, though, certainly, other contemporary poets have done so. I suppose the influence in my case to be more basic than the choice of actual biblical subject matter; it is really a fundamental attitude toward experience, in which the moral sense and the dramatic sense are fused into one thing. Many years of reading, study, and writing have made a difference in how I respond to Genesis, too, so that its ways of acting on me have become more conscious, affecting my sense of how structure and detail cooperate in a literary (and mythic) narrative. It is this adult, analytical understanding of scripture that I want to bring to the story of Lot.

———————

The stories of Genesis echo, overlap, and bleed into each other—as, in fact, do separate poems in a well-composed volume of poetry. Lot's story is, first of all, involved in the much

more central narrative concerning Abraham. Abraham's
brother Haran was Lot's father, which makes Abraham Lot's
uncle. He is also Lot's better, the patriarch who founds the line
of God's Israel, which Lot does *not* engender. As their story begins, however, they are very close; nephew follows uncle down
into Egypt during one of Canaan's famines (a theme later
echoed in the Joseph story); but then they return together and
continue to prosper as herdsmen in Canaan. Lot is a good man,
and yet not quite good enough, as chapter 13 quickly demonstrates: the consolidated flocks having grown too large for available pasturage, Abraham proposes a separation of goods and
generously (or because he already knows how Lot will react?)
allows Lot to choose which territory will be his. Lot chooses the
Vale of Siddim (or, as it is most often translated, the Plain of
Jordan, adjacent to the Salt—or Dead—Sea). Indeed, he goes to
Sodom, one of the "Cities of the Circle," traditionally known as
the "Cities of the Plain." (In a more accurate transliteration,
Sodom is "Sedom," which is the form this essay will use.) No
doubt the grass looked greener in the Salt Sea Valley; but
Canaan was the Land chosen by God as the place where the divine blessing would flourish. Lot ignored that covenantal truth
and, looking at the Vale of Siddim, moist and green as it was,
compared it to "the Lord's own garden," and, beside that, to
Egypt. But Egypt in the Bible is never a good place. At best, it
serves as a fallback when famine strikes the Promised Land. No
matter: Lot betook himself to Sedom, which in Hebrew means
"burnt," another sign of what awaited him there.

Trouble first comes in the form of an invasion from a ruler
named Chedorlaomer, who takes a number of Sedom's inhabitants captive, Lot among them. Chapter 14 shows us Abraham
in an unaccustomed guise, as a military leader, strong enough
to save his nephew. The patriarch and his men defeat Chedorlaomer and return Lot unharmed to his adopted city. Some
time after, Abraham engages in skillful bartering with Yahweh,

who eventually agrees to spare Sedom if a minimum of ten faithful people can be mustered there. (Is this the origin— along with the fact of the Commandments numbering ten—of the minyan, Judaism's traditional requirement that there must be a quorum of ten congregants in order to hold any religious service?) Alas, Abraham didn't go quite far enough with his bargaining. If he had persuaded God that the lives of four righteous people were sufficient reason to spare the city, the story would have gone differently—actually, there wouldn't have been much story at all. Lot doesn't seem to have had any missionary instincts. Apparently no one except him, his wife, and two daughters knew and served the Lord. The rest, abandoned to their ignorance, were pagans. The same applied to another of the Circle Cities, Gomorrah (or, in another transliteration, "Amora"), which, like Sedom (or Sodom), had been sending up "a great noise of sin" to Heaven. The result is that God is moved to destroy all these sinks of iniquity in the Valley. Indeed, this valley was a landscape visually appropriate as a site for sinful cities, since it abounded in pits of asphalt (or bitumen), rather like the La Brea tar pits of Los Angeles. Actually, bitumen is quite flammable, and this fact has allowed modern science to propose a purely rational explanation for the incineration of the Jordan Plain recounted in Genesis. But Lot lives in Sedom, not in the other cities, and it is while God is on his way there to number the faithful that Abraham argues for Sedom's salvation.

Not Yahweh as such, but instead two representative angels (or messengers) arrive in Sedom, indistinguishable from ordinary mortals except, perhaps, by a fascinating, elusive radiance. Lot, who is sitting just inside the town gate, seems to recognize what sort of beings he is encountering, for he bows his head to the ground, addresses them as "lords," and invites them to stop a night with him. At first they refuse, saying they prefer to sleep outside by the road; but Lot prevails. Their first choice, staying outdoors like shepherds and nomads, would in biblical terms be preferable to putting up in a house in the city of Sedom. Agrarian societies and the conurbations that build up around them are always inferior in Hebrew sacred story to the cooper- ative (in contemporary terms, socialist) life of nomads. This perspective is first suggested in the account of Cain and Abel, where the grain and fruit offered in sacrifice by Cain (a farmer) are disdained by God in favor of the firstlings from the flock tended by his brother Abel (a shepherd). Archetypal murder results, which predicts the future course of Cain's descendants. A second variation on the theme occurs in the story of Babel, where the building of a city tower is viewed by Yahweh as a prideful breach of the distance between humankind and God. To this, God puts a bizarre end by the expedient of replacing the original universal language with the "babel" of many tongues. Among the many things we find in the story is a mythological working out of a chronic truth about urbanism—that cities inevitably attract foreigners eager to engage in trade. Speaking different languages, however, they are unable to cooperate. Finally, cities attract invaders, as we saw when Chedorlaomer invaded Sedom and took Lot captive.

––––––––––

But Lot has decided to remain in his city, in his immovable house, and after some entreaty the angels accept the invitation to lodge there with him. The best-known incident in Lot's story quickly follows: Sedom's townsmen gather at his door and ask to have the wondrous visitors brought outside and made available for sexual relations. The Hebrew is clear about their intentions. In Sedom men seem to expect to have sexual relations with men—a regular feature, apparently, of urban life. The mistake would be to understand this practice as "the sin of Sodom." It is only *one* of Sodom's sins, in biblical understanding. Yet it would be taken very seriously as that by nomadic herdsmen, a people moving about from place to place according to the seasons, living barely above subsistence level, with high infant mortality rates and fear of attacks from roving bandits or predatory animals. In such societies, every child is a great and incomparable blessing, and no practice interfering with the regular and constant engendering of children can be tolerated. That would include the practice of sexual relations with a wife during menstruation, which Leviticus 20:18 also forbids in searing terms. Five verses earlier in Leviticus, the notorious proscription of male-to-male relations appears, with its concurrent assignment of the death penalty for the said offense—which, in fact, is also assigned for adultery and incest. Actually, the whole of Leviticus 20 ought to be read by anyone proposing to base modern law on biblical sources. For why accept one of these proscriptions and penalties without accepting them all?

No mention of male-to-male relations is made concerning Amora, which nevertheless suffers a rain of fire and brimstone for its sins, too. We can assume that Sedom's sister city embodied the usual urban conditions that make an Egypt out of the Lord's garden, without the unintentionally comic assertion sometimes made that Amora's sin was lesbianism. In any case, Lot's adopted city exhibits a sufficient sinfulness, apart from the sexual practices of his townspeople, to invoke God's wrath. Because no matter the sexes involved, what the men outside his door are pushing for is rape—and beyond that, a violation of the laws of hospitality, one of the ancient world's most sacred taboos. The grave nature of this taboo (along with Lot's awareness that his guests are angels) is the only mitigation of the story's next and most appalling plot turn. In a desperate effort to dissuade the mob outside his door from raping his guests, Lot offers to send his daughters out to them as sexual surrogates. This is not one of the Bible's shining examples of what are now called "family values."

The mob refuses the offer and even begins to threaten Lot himself with rape, at which point the angelic messengers snatch him back inside the house and beam a flash of blinding light at the attackers so that the latter can no longer even find the door to Lot's house. In a nearly universal symbol-system, one's house is one's person, so the assault on Lot's door is, symbolically, an effort to penetrate his body. Moreover, in Freudian terms, to be blinded is to be castrated, which of course would be one way to disarm a mob of rapists. But light in the Bible is always also enlightenment, even when, as here, it takes a violent form. The angels' lightning-flash also prefigures the rain of fire soon to descend on Sedom, fulfilling the implicit prophecy encoded in its name.

The messengers urge Lot to leave Sedom, taking his wife and two daughters with him. At first he balks, and only after the angels seize his hand and drag him forward does he agree to this mini-Exodus. (And later readers were, perhaps only unconsciously, to understand it as an exodus, if only because of the clue that the meal Lot offers to his guests includes unleavened bread. The book of Genesis was assembled, of course, centuries after the events in Exodus occurred, which allowed for any number of foreshadowings of things to come in Torah.) Character is destiny, Heraclitus says, and so we can't be too surprised when Lot dismisses the angels' recommendation of fleeing to the hills. Instead of the traditional habitat of the nomadic shepherd, Lot insists on making for a small city nearby. A conflation of the angelic messengers with God himself begins at verse 17 of the nineteenth chapter, where use of the pronoun "they" is immediately followed by a "he" referring to the voice of divine authority. Verse 18 contains one more "them," but then the angels drop out of the story and thereafter, Lot speaks directly to God. God grants Lot his variance, dispensing him from a retreat into the hills, and says he will make an exception for the town he has chosen in the general destruction of the Circle Cities. Thereafter the spared town will be called Zoar, which in Hebrew means "small." A contemporary equivalent might be "Littleton," and if we probe the story for mythicized content, perhaps the inference to draw is that small towns are less subject to serious vices than large urban conglomerations. Yet surely the difference is strictly comparative, as the citizens of Peyton Place might tell us.

Although Lot is spared the "atomic" destruction of Sedom, he still hasn't made the best possible choice. The first disaster is the one befalling his wife (never named in the story), who ignores or forgets God's injunction, pronounced in verse 17, that neither Lot nor any member of his family should look back at Sedom. We may wonder whether his wife succumbs to the temptation because she is curious to see flames consuming the city, or whether she wants one last view of a home where she has been happy. The account doesn't say, but it does present the startling detail of her being turned into a pillar of salt. Recent commentary has pointed out that the terrain around the Dead Sea is dotted with strange mineral formations, and that folk traditions thereabouts regarded these "pillars of salt" as remains of people who had seen God. But such traditions don't explain the relevance of this mysterious incident. Reading for implicit meanings apart from simple narrative surprise, we might begin by comparing the story to the Orpheus myth, in which Orpheus loses his wife to the underworld because *he* looks back to see whether she is still following him as they are climbing up to light and life. He confirms that she is indeed there just at the moment when he loses her forever—which even so leads to his own fullest achievement as a player of the lyre, singer, and poet, during the short period left to him before he is in turn killed. A saying of Jesus' (Luke 9:62) might be adduced as well. When a potential follower says he would like to join the disciples and will do so as soon as he has had a chance to bid his family farewell, Jesus replies, "No man, having put his hand to the plough, and looking back, is fit for the kingdom of God." Many proverbial statements warn us never to look back, whether or not the Jordan Valley's pillar of salt is explicitly invoked. For what's done is done, regrets are useless, salt tears do nothing to change the past, and God never destroys the order of time by making it run in reverse.

Abraham is, on the other hand, allowed to witness the destruction of Sedom and Amora (verses twenty-seven and twenty-eight), and the smoke rising above them looks to him like smoke from a furnace (or kiln), just as it did (yet another echo) in the account of Abraham's first sacrifice of animals in 15:17. Some modern readers coming upon these lines will be reminded of the smoke that hovered over Auschwitz and Buchenwald, after Nazi authority had determined to enact a perversion of biblical tradition by arresting Jewish citizens in Germany (and in the lands subjugated by Germany) and destroying them. They also targeted other insufficiently Aryan people like gypsies, along with their own latter-day "sodomites." A main obstacle to commemorating the torture and murder of innocent people in the camps under the name "Holocaust" is that the latter word originally referred to a burnt offering to God, performed by a priest or proto-priest like Noah, Melchizedek, or Abraham. That is why the word "Shoah," Hebrew for "catastrophe," has been proposed as an alternative term designating the twentieth century's worst moment. To the extent that the Nazis regarded their genocide as a holy deed, they were, in their own minds, performing a "holocaust." To later observers, these events can only be seen as a horrible parody, yet one all too present in consciousness when contemporary bigotry arrogates to itself the role of God as sole judge of humankind and consigns those deemed sinful to Hell fire.

At this point Abraham drops out of Lot's story; no further contact between them is recorded. Lot has gone to Zoar, but once there he becomes fearful; the story doesn't say what has frightened him. In any case, he retreats to the hills with his daughters and hides in a cave. But it is too late, and the final wretched incident in Lot's story unfolds. The elder daughter decides that their hermit's life offers no opportunity for either sister ever to marry, which means that Lot's line will come to an end. She persuades the younger sister to join her in a plan to trick their father. They give him too much wine, he becomes drunk, and then, on two successive nights, each daughter has incestuous relations with him. The story never says so, yet, in my mind, this hideous deception on their part is linked to Lot's earlier proposal of sending his daughters out to the mob in Sedom, which they can't have failed to hear. In the deplorable economy of retribution, Lot is here being repaid. We are never given, in the story, any of Lot's reactions once he learns the truth—for what could he possibly say? Both daughters bear children, the elder a son she names Moab, the younger a son she names Ben-Ammi. Lot's line does continue; but from Moab springs the Moabites, and from Ben-Ammi the Ammonites, neither people destined to become servants of Israel's God.

There has already occurred a strange foreshadowing of this instance of misengendering. It comes in Noah's story when, immediately after the Flood, Noah plants a vineyard (9:20), becoming, according to this verse, "the first tiller of the soil," in direct contradiction to the description of Cain in 4:2. Here, too, the disadvantages of agriculture are underlined: one agricultural product is the grape, which can be used to make wine. Noah becomes drunk and falls asleep naked in his tent, after which his son Ham comes to him and "saw his nakedness," a phrase, in Hebrew, equivalent to actual sexual contact. Ham's brothers manage to cover their father with a blanket without looking at him, with the result that their lineage is blessed, while Ham's is cursed ever after to be servants of his brothers' descendants. When I was a child growing up in southern Geor-

gia, this passage was cited as a proof text explaining why it was
that Africans and their American descendants had "always"
been slaves to other races: Ham was the ancestor of all black
Africans, it was asserted. Therefore we needn't feel bad if all
our servants were black and we paid them slave wages. This is
one more tragic instance of how the clear sense of God's universal love for the human race that he created, as recorded in
the Bible, has been distorted by a parody of biblical argumen-
tation to justify what cannot be justified.

The similarity between Ham's and Lot's story is unmistak-
able, particularly as it has to do with lineage and misgender-
ing. Genesis stresses the importance of right generation, and
one way of stressing it is to show how engendering can go
wrong. Lot provides a cautionary tale of misengendering. Irre-
deemable misengendering, forever and ever? Well, perhaps not
forever. Later Judaic tradition expressly forbade intermarriage
with the Moabites, who were settled in territories adjacent to
the Promised Land. And yet, as we know, that proscription was
ignored by Naomi's sons, who came to Moab and took local
wives. True enough, they died there, without offspring. The
moving part of the story comes when the widow of one of
them decides to follow Naomi back to Canaan and give up her
Moabite identity, a decision with a beautiful sequel. This
widow, Ruth, marries her husband's kinsman Boaz, gives birth
to Obed, the father of Jesse, who was the father of David. So a
Moabite was thus the distant ancestor not only of Judah's great
warrior king, but also of the Messiah, who must come from
David's line. Ultimately the Messiah's ancestry can be traced
back to the misengendering of Lot's daughters—which makes
this story a prime example of God's transformation of human
misdeeds into rungs of a ladder up to heaven. Just so, Jacob's
defrauding of his brother Esau, after a series of trials, is made
good; God eventually ascribes Jacob's heritage to Israel, the
people who bear the second name given to him.

How often it's true that the stories of the Bible are stories of "good saves," worked out after the characters in a given narrative have gone astray. As such, the stories offer hope to all of us who, time after time, have made wrong choices. The Bible, and Genesis in particular, demonstrates that God has the power, over time, to bring good out of its opposite. This is not the same as saying that the end justifies the means. To begin with, there is no end: the story of God's people is still going on. In the process, or task, of making good come from evil, one key seems to be resolving not to dwell too much on the past (which always risks turning us into a pillar of salt), but instead looking forward to discern how our "save" is going to work out.

Still, I want to pause a moment here to look back to my childhood, with its constant Bible reading and frequent inculcation of wrong and harmful doctrine. At some point I was led to understand the story of Sedom as having to do with the sexuality that was mine—an orientation that, instead of choosing, I *discovered,* without anyone's calling it to my attention. It really was the "love that dare not speak its name," and certainly no one ever spoke it in my earshot. An orientation I discovered, kept secret, and then fought against with all my power, beginning around age twelve and on through high school and the first years of college. I believed I was in danger of the "sin of Sodom," which was being sent my way as some sort of temptation from Satan, to be countered with constant prayer and anxious recourse to Christian hope. Nothing availed. At last, I abandoned religious faith altogether on the basis of the following reasoning: "Doctrine tells me God created me as I am, and it also tells me that the way I am is sinful. I have faithfully called upon God to change the way I am and He hasn't done so. Because God hasn't changed me, I am condemned to Hell fire for all eternity. Yet a God who would ordain such unjust and cruel conditions for so many of His children [by then

I had read up on my situation and knew I wasn't alone] is not
a God I can love or worship or even believe in. Therefore I relinquish the faith that was taught to me and will lead from
now on a secular life."

This reasoning still seems sound to me, and what I see in it
is the basic sense of justice fostered by the Bible and religious
tradition itself, which teach that we cannot serve an evil master. Where I was mistaken was in the assumption that God
considers same-sex relations sinful for all time. A study of the
Bible and religious tradition in their relationship to an evolv-
ing system of ethics stands behind the revised view. Humankind has forged onward in vast distances from its origins as a
nomadic, hunter-gatherer-herdsman polity. If that was paradise, it has been lost. Agriculture, property ownership, urbanism, and all that follows from them are inescapable facts of
human life for the majority of those now living. New conditions call for new decisions; far from being essential for survival of the race, human fertility has become a threat to civilization. Population projections for the twenty-first century are
truly terrifying to contemplate. All of this may be the result of
wrong choices made in early phases of our history, but the resulting conditions are what they are. God does not set time
running backward.

Nor, I believe, has God abandoned to chaos those who know
themselves to be God's children. We possess overall guidelines
spelled out clearly in the Bible, guidelines that have not
changed; but the regulation of the detail of conduct is different
from its early formulations, in keeping with altered conditions,
both bad and good, that history has wrought. The role that
women play in contemporary society, to bring in only one example, is radically different from its biblical counterpart, and
only a small number of women would look back to that world
with longing. The promises implicitly and explicitly made in
the Judaeo-Christian tradition necessarily preclude any dogged

perpetuation of the penalties in Leviticus, which are condoned only by those for whom Scripture's value is inseparable from literal readings. In place of a letter-of-the-law acceptation of the Bible, I recommend an alternative, an overview in which we catch the essential gist of sacred story. In this perspective, God is loving and merciful, not an angry deity lying in wait to punish us. God's name (as given to Moses in Exodus 3:14) can be translated "I will be as I will be," and this God, who acts in history, expects humankind to participate in a continuing creation. The congregation of the faithful does so by accepting the divine order so as to engender a just society.

Confusions and wrongdoings of the modern world do not have to be the final word; nor are we inescapably doomed to wars raining down destructive fires on the nations of the earth—even if all of them are overrun with greed and crime as much ever as the Cities of the Circle. A "good save" is still possible for our overwhelming problems, but it will require an enormous effort by all people concerned, one not at all likely in the absence of faith. Just possibly part of the solution will come from those writers—and there are a surprising number of them now—who work to lend a sacred dimension to experience. Their example will be useful to readers of good will learning to understand their own biographies as part of the larger salvational narrative. When they experience that organic connection, the next step is to act on the truth that they have come to see.

The Story of
Abraham
and Sarah

Phillip Lopate

A border incident. Abraham, like many travelers, is worried about being stopped and detained by customs guards for bringing something into the country—in this case, the beauty of his wife. So he passes off Sarah as his sister, to save his own life, and she is brought to Pharaoh as a playmate, and Pharaoh, well pleased with her, rewards her "brother" with wealth. Then God intervenes and Sarah is given back to her rightful husband. A scandalous story, one of the most unnerving in the Bible: even if you do not accept Abraham as "ignoble," as does Harold Bloom, at the very least he seems dishonest. Later, Abraham repeats the ruse in Gerar, and this time Sarah becomes the consort of King Abimelach.[1] (The scenario is repeated a third time in Genesis, when copycat son Isaac palms off Rebekah as his sister to the same, incorrigibly gullible, Abimelach.)

Taken together, these three episodes are referred to by scholars as the "wife-sister stories." Though I am no Bible scholar, the stories intrigue me. My plan for this essay is: (1) to examine the ways that the experts—rabbis, folklorists, anthropologists, literary critics—have written about the wife-sister stories; (2) to consider the psychological viewpoint of Karen Horney and Sigmund Freud on incest, intimacy, and marriage; and (3) to narrate an episode from my own past that I associate, rightly or wrongly, with the Bible tale. I hope to line up all three perspectives like images in a stereopticon, each superimposing over the others to produce a more three-dimensional quandariness.

Abraham and Sarah

Rabbinical commentators have labored to put a positive spin on Abraham's deception. The customary approach in the Middle Ages was to vilify the other nations as barbarians—accentuating their bloodthirsty and lecherous tendencies, thereby justifying Abraham's fears.[2] The commentators were not above racism, as when one elucidating legend, or midrash, has Abraham warn Sarah, "'now we are about to enter a country whose inhabitants are black-skinned, and therefore your beauty will be all the more conspicuous.' Compared to Sarah's beauty, all other women were as monkeys" (*The Midrash Says,* selected by Rabbi Moshe Weissman).

One classic rabbinical commentary imagines Abraham going much further to protect Sarah than the terse account in Genesis. In this version, the tax collectors ask Abraham about the contents of his casket, and Abraham says: barley. No, it must be wheat, they say. Okay, I'll pay the tax on wheat. The exchange keeps escalating, until he volunteers to pay the taxes for precious jewels and gold, at which point they demand the casket be opened, and see the ravishing Sarah.

Not all the rabbis exonerate Abraham, however. The great Rambam (Nachmanides) unequivocally says: "Know that

Abraham our father unintentionally committed a great sin by bringing his righteous wife to a stumbling-block of sin on account of his fear for his life. He should have trusted that G-d would save him and his wife and all his belongings for G-d surely has the power to help and save."

Somewhere between Rambam and the vindicators lies the analysis of Radak (in Nahum Sarna's paraphrase):

> Abram was confronted with a moral dilemma, forced to make a choice between two evils. If he discloses the truth he will be killed, and his wife, beautiful and unprotected in an alien society of low morality, will assuredly be condemned to a life of shame and abuse. If, however, he resorts to subterfuge, she may be violated by some Egyptian, but at least husband and wife would both survive. It would have been improper, then, to have relied on a miracle as an excuse for inaction.

Even if we grant Radak's defense, why the need to repeat the story? Surely if a patriarch's actions look dubious the first time, our uneasiness can only increase when the story is thrice told. The formalist, lit-crit answer is that reiteration was a "desirable and characteristic feature of the epic tradition" (Sarna). We are still left with fitting this strange piece of behavior into the rest of Abraham's biography.

Let us take a closer look at our protagonist. A nonconformist, God-haunted man, he leaves the safety of his home at a word from the Deity, wanders like a "discontent" (Bloom's term) here and there, temporarily loses his wife by pretending she is his sister, shows reluctance to send away his second wife, Hagar, makes land deals and grows wealthy, tries unsuccessfully to stop God from destroying Sodom, comes close to sacrificing his beloved son Isaac because God told him to, grieves when his wife Sarah dies, and remarries (according to one midrash, going back to Hagar). Vacillating one moment, zealously rigid the next, cowardly and brave, the quintessential father figure (as his name change from Abram to Abraham indicates) who nevertheless takes eighty years to sire a child, he seems all the more sympathetic to me for his inconsistencies.

It is tempting to compare Abraham to Odysseus. Both are wily survivors. But it is hard to imagine Odysseus hiding behind a woman—or loaning Penelope to a foreign potentate. Odysseus is more a man of action and physical prowess, the classic hero, whereas Abraham is "aheroic" and "belongs to the paradigm of the fool" (to borrow Peter Pitzele's terms). On the other hand, as Pitzele notes in *Our Fathers' Wells*, Abraham is a visionary, with a power of spiritual obedience and an inward, listening quality that Odysseus utterly lacks. Odysseus would never wander the globe at an instigation as vague as the call of God. And nothing Odysseus does is as noble, finally, as Abraham's expostulating with God to save the people of Sodom, trying to bargain the Almighty Himself into compassion.

The folklorists see the wife-sister stories as a variant of popular tales about the hero's beautiful wife who faces being kidnapped by a rival prince, and who proves faithful or unfaithful (Helen of Troy, for instance). One difference between the Greek epics and Genesis, however, is that often the Bible figures are made to appear less heroic, the better to demonstrate God's power. It is God alone, not her husband, who can protect Sarah, by inflicting plagues and boils (read: sexual dysfunction) on Pharaoh, and by sewing up the wombs of the Gerarites so that no one in the land can get pregnant.

The wife-sister stories also allow the biblical authors to crow about the beauty of their matriarch (all the more miraculous when you consider she is well past eighty!). I like the midrash that says Abraham was so modest he had never before observed how lovely Sarah was. But, says Rambam, "Wading through a stream, he saw the reflection of her beauty in the water." Very delicate, almost Japanese. It suggests a haiku:

Crossing into Egypt
River mirrors wife's appeal
They're gonna kill me!

As it turns out, Abraham lives and prospers by becoming Sarah's booking agent, you might say. ("Pander" is too strong a word.)

When Pharaoh bombards Abraham with rhetorical questions ("What is this you have done to me! Why did you not tell me that she was your wife? Why did you say, 'She is my sister,' so that I took her as my wife?"), the patriarch makes no reply. A modern reader may agree that Pharaoh has a point. The ruler had acted in good faith, showing generosity toward the sojourner; it seems unjust for God to punish the Egyptians, when Abraham misled them. Later, when the story repeats at Gerar, King Abimelach addresses Abraham in tones similar to Pharaoh's: "'What have you done to us? What wrong have I done that you should bring so great a guilt upon me and my kingdom? You have done to me things that ought not to be done. What, then,' Abimelach demanded of Abraham, 'was your purpose in doing this thing?'"

It is worth wondering what the biblical authors had in mind by putting such rhetorically persuasive passages into the mouths of the non-Jews. Abimelach's questions are too direct to be avoided; this time Abraham must speak up, and he does. Source analysts, in fact, argue that one of the reasons why the E writer repeats the story that J has already written is precisely to give Abraham a chance to defend himself the second time around. So the E writer's variant takes much greater pains to show that Sarah's virtue was untainted—that Abimelach never got a chance to sleep with her—while the earlier, Egyptian episode by the J writer is less reassuring on this score. In *The Book of J*, Harold Bloom sees such distinctions as proof that J is the more terse, impious storyteller ("J has no particular affection for her patriarchs"), while E is "characteristically . . . prissier."

The only problem with this reading is that in some ways Abraham comes off looking worse in the Gerar episode than in the Egyptian one. The first time, he may be excused by the novelty of fear; the second time begins to look like Metternichian policy. Devora Steinmetz, in her book *From Father to Son,* argues that Abraham's motivation for going to Gerar was initially weaker (no famine); and there was more at stake the second time in letting Sarah become another man's wife. Since God had already promised Sarah she would become pregnant soon, the paternity of the heir and the whole blood-line might be compromised.

Moreover, Abraham's spoken defense, when it comes, is not that impressive. As Devora Steinmetz observes, "He . . . gives more than one explanation, which suggests that no one explanation was good enough." In fact, he gives three explanations: (1) "I thought . . . surely there is no fear of God in this place, and they will kill me because of my wife." We have no way of knowing how reasonable was this apprehension, since no records exist to substantiate the frequency of such criminal practices among the Gerarites. But we do know that Abimelach demonstrates plenty of fear of God, after the Deity comes to him in a dream and warns him not to touch Sarah. (2) Next, Abraham utters the surprising statement, "And besides, she is in truth my sister, my father's daughter though not my mother's; and she became my wife." Now, no previous genealogies in Genesis suggest so close a kinship between Abraham and Sarah. Either he is improvising a yarn, which makes him a liar, or he is telling the truth, which convicts him of incest.

Some of the rabbinical commentators believe that he is merely throwing sand in the heathen's eyes. Modern apologists have even argued that because the Israelites were "underdogs," they had the right to practice deception, as part of a "trickster" culture. Somehow this does not sit right: mendacity justified by minority status.

Supposing, however, that Abraham is telling the truth, and Sarah *is* his half-sister. One anthropological defense has it that, while incest was certainly taboo in Abraham's day, the prohibition may not have held as strongly then between half-siblings. There is also the elaborate argument of Ephraim Speiser in the Genesis volume of the Anchor Bible, among others (based on some hazy fragments of Nuzi tablets), that Abraham was only following a common practice borrowed from the neighboring Hurrians, to "marry a girl and adopt her at the same time as his sister." Adin Steinsaltz, the contemporary Talmudist, takes a similar approach to Speiser's in his book *Biblical Images:*

> Moreover *sister* was a common term of endearment for a woman in early Eastern cultures; for instance, in the Song of Songs, we find "My sister, my spouse" (5:1) and "My sister, my love.". . . The sister-wife was the chief wife, as opposed to the other, secondary wives who were "outsiders."

I find this whole line of thinking beside the point. The story's power lies precisely in the fact that Abraham is frightened for his life, and so asks Sarah to pretend they are brother and sister. If Abraham is not lying when he asks Sarah to say they are brother and sister, but only invoking an honorific, the story goes from being filled with tension and guilt to sitcom misunderstanding. Devora Steinmetz puts it well: "Even if, as some have suggested, Abraham's claim refers to a specific type of aristocratic marriage . . . Sarah is still Abraham's wife, and Abimelach is not free to take her." I also like Rambam's commentary: "Even if it were true that she was his sister and his wife, nevertheless when they wanted to take her as a wife and he told them, *She is my sister,* in order to lead them astray, he already committed a sin towards them by bringing upon them

a *great sin,* and it no longer mattered at all whether the thing
was true or false!"

Then Abraham produces his final excuse. (3) "So when God
made me wander from my father's house, I said to her, 'Let this
be the kindness that you shall do me: whatever place we come
to, say there of me: He is my brother.'" If the first part of Abraham's statement sounds like a whiny attempt to shift the blame
onto God, the second part is, for me, the crux of the matter: he
admits that not only did this deception occur at Egypt and
Gerar, but it was their regular practice. They were like scam
artists using the same brother-sister masquerade in each town.

And what of Sarah's feelings in all this? Ilona Roshkow, in
her indignant book *The Phallacy of Genesis,* views the wife-
sister story as a paradigm of "powerful male/powerless fe-
male/uninvited sex." She points to Sarah's "silence" as evidence
of her being treated as chattel (although elsewhere, I must say,
Sarah has no problem opening up her mouth: she objects
loudly to her rival Hagar's presence, and "laughs" at God for
telling her she will conceive). Roshkow indicts biblical sexism:
"The irony is that Pharaoh, Abimelach, and I as a reader understand the immorality of adultery, and the crime of female
sexual sacrifice, more readily than Abraham."

Adin Steinsaltz takes the opposite tack, reading into Sarah's
silence a noble, communitarian maturity:

> This silence did not arise from passivity or surrender, nor from
> a wish to be taken by another man, nor because Sarah was a
> mere tool of her husband: her acquiescence was obviously pre-
> arranged with Abraham, with whom she worked as a team on
> the basis of decisions jointly made. Here, they had decided, de-
> spite the shame and humiliation involved, that it was preferable
> to preserve the wholeness of Abraham's camp—representing, as
> it did, the new ideal—even at the cost of Sarah's honor. This
> willingness to sacrifice her personal well-being for the common

cause is surely borne out by the fact that Sarah never reproached Abraham for the injury done to her; nor, indeed, did she even mention it.

To Steinsaltz, we may take Sarah's silence for consent; to Roshkow, the opposite. There is no end to the moral judgments we can make of the characters in these stories. Myself, I have little inclination to judge Abraham—or Sarah. What interests me is the fluid way this couple keeps crossing the line between spouse and sibling, and what that indicates in a larger sense about the condition of marriage.

Sigmund and Karen

The first time I consciously took in the story of Abraham passing off Sarah as his sister, I felt—not disgust but a shiver of identification. I could identify with Abraham's faintheartedness, since I am not a brave man myself, and might resort to any pusillanimous strategies to save my neck. But there was something more to the shock of recognition, something uncannily personal, as though I had once done the same but could not remember when. It was the same sensation as when I've dreamt that I've already killed a man, or already married my mother or slept with my sister, and now must sort out the aftermath of that abomination.

I thought of a passage I'd once read in Karen Horney's essay "The Problem of the Monogamous Ideal." One of the reasons people marry, wrote Horney, is to fulfill "all the old desires arising out of the Oedipal situation in childhood." But the increasing intimacy within marriage leads to

> a resuscitation of the old incest prohibition—this time in relation to the marriage partner, and the more complete the fulfillment of unconscious wishes, the greater is the danger. The revival of the incest prohibition in marriage is apparently very

typical and leads *mutatis mutandis* to the same results as in the relation between child and parent; that is, the direct sexual aims give place to an affectionate attitude in which the sexual aim is inhibited.

The way I remembered this passage was that even (or especially) in good marriages, where the partners communicate, there is a tendency to begin as lovers and end up as brothers and sisters.

Now, perhaps Horney's formulation is merely a psychoanalytic restatement of the age-old folk wisdom that marriage is the surest way to kill off sexual passion. The Talmud itself tells us: "Since the destruction of the Temple, sexual pleasure has been taken away from those who practice it lawfully and given to sinners, as it is written: 'Stolen waters are sweet, and bread eaten in secret is pleasant.'" What Horney contributes to this sour truism is an explanation: that the decrease of sexual pleasure in marriage comes about not merely via habit but because of a revival of the incest prohibition. It is almost as though one were revirginated by closeness—or as though intimacy itself carried with it the stigma of familial trespass.

Although the incestuous aura projected onto the spouse could be Oedipal, I chose to see it in the light of siblings—of wives becoming rounded off into sisters, or husbands, brothers. Most likely, this "sibling" reading of the passage came from the fact that I grew up with two sisters. They were both younger than I, and, as it happens, pretty and sexy, and each could not help but figure in the development of my erotic imagination. For instance, my sisters are both brunette, slender, about five-foot-five—a type I have consistently fallen for. So for me to say that the wife becomes a sister-figure is not entirely to rob her of a sexual dimension. Far from it: one difference between the conjugal and the brother-sister tie may be that the latter, unconsummated, never loses its erotic edge.

To return to this question of the "affectionate attitude in
which the sexual aim is inhibited." Horney acknowledges her
debt to a well-known paper by Freud, called "The Most Prevalent Form of Degradation in Erotic Life," in which he analyzes
the tendency of many men to suffer a polarized split between
affection and sexual desire. "Where such men love they have
no desire and where they desire they cannot love," declared
Freud. Inhibited by the incest taboo, and over-esteeming their
well-brought-up mothers and sisters, they can only be potent
"when the sexual object fulfills the condition of being degraded," either because the woman comes from a lower class or
has loose morals. Just as important, she "does not know the
rest of his life and cannot criticize him" for "perverse" sexual
longings. "It is to such a woman that he prefers to devote his
sexual potency, even when all the tenderness in him belongs to
a higher type."

The modern bourgeois male may no longer have as developed a courtesan demi-monde to turn to as the nineteenth-
century type Freud was describing, but I think much of what
he says holds true—else why the need for the *Playboy* Channel?
Freud concludes with a breathtakingly audacious assertion:
"whoever is to be really free and happy in love must have overcome his deference for women and come to terms with the
idea of incest with mother or sister."

Interestingly enough, Freud refers to Genesis in this essay: "A
man shall leave father and mother—according to Biblical precept—and cleave to his wife." Now, to return to our wife-sister
story: Sarah is the mother-figure in Genesis, the Matriarch of
Israel. Moreover, she is getting on in years—close to ninety, so
the text tells us; even if we consider the figure an exaggeration
and halve it, she has definitely entered her matronly period.
Somehow the shadow of "mother-incest" will have to be lifted
or diffused for the marriage to revive. Curiously, Sarah is also
barren: her greatest suffering is that she is *not* a mother. She

urges on Abraham her servant girl, Hagar, and with this "less exalted sexual object," as Freud would put it, he regains his potency—that is, fathers a child. This, in turn, awakens Sarah's jealousy and her power as a woman.

Theirs is, in a sense, an open marriage: just as Sarah tempts Abraham into infidelity by giving him Hagar, so Abraham lets his wife be taken over by strangers. That their marriage has lost some of its oomph and needs replenishment is suggested by the episode when Sarah laughs, scornfully, at the promise of childbirth: "Now that I am withered, am I to have enjoyment—with my husband so old?" She does not expect her old codger of a husband to be able to pleasure her.[3] You could say, then, that they are keeping the sexual roots of their marriage alive, by playing taboo roles (you be the sister, I'll be the brother).

It seems odd that, at the moment Abraham erotically awakens to his wife's comeliness, he de-sexualizes her by giving her the role of sister. On the other hand, one could argue, following Freud's model, that he reinvests her with even more sexual interest, by placing her in a compromising position, where she becomes the plaything of another man, thereby whetting his jealousy.

In another essay, "A Special Type of Object Choice Made by Men," Freud wrote that, with certain men:

> a virtuous and reputable woman never possesses the charm required to exalt her to an object of love; this attraction is exercised only by one who is more or less sexually discredited, whose fidelity and loyalty admit of some doubt. . . . Not until they have some occasion for jealousy does their passion reach its height and the woman acquire her full value to them.

You might say that Abraham forces this most faithful of wives to play the role of a courtesan, a light woman, as a means of sexually re-charging their marriage. By the way, I am not seriously maintaining that this is what happened, or that Abraham was so motivated; for all I know, there may never have even been an historical Abraham. I am only suggesting that these undercurrents, brought into the open, make the story come alive for me.

Let me turn, by comparison, to a modern variant of the wife-sister story: Paul Bowles's novel, *The Sheltering Sky.* In *The Sheltering Sky,* Port and Kit have been married for twelve years and have evolved into a sort of brother-sister duo. ("'Like two children,' he thought, 'who aren't being allowed to go on a picnic with the family.'") They have long since stopped making love, but they are dependent on each other, and Kit feels convinced that Port could not be interested in any other woman. (Actually, he makes love to an Arab prostitute, a "degraded sexual object," in Freud's terminology, unbeknownst to Kit.) Port is a wanderer, like Abraham, and he, too, places his wife in danger, by traveling through North Africa with a very handsome acquaintance of theirs, Tunner. But he rationalizes that she is faithful ("What the hell, he'll never get her"). Actually, Kit does end up sleeping with Tunner. Port is also afraid, like Abraham, of the alien culture through which he is traveling, and this fear motivates a good deal of his behavior: "'I wonder if after all I'm a coward?' he thought. Fear spoke; he listened and let it persuade—the classical procedure." Port also places Kit (and himself) in danger, albeit unconsciously, by traveling to a place without adequate medical facilities, and then falling gravely ill. After he dies, she is ravished by Bedouins and lets herself become their sexual prisoner.

Port and Kit represent the nightmarish turn that might have happened to Abraham and Sarah, without God's intervention. As it is, the biblical couple suffer a multitude of troubles—barrenness, periodic separations, wife/mistress tensions, brother-in-law problems—and somehow hold together as a couple. To what extent does their ability to modulate into siblings, as protective coloration, facilitate this conjugal longevity? Perhaps they are only following the example of their ancestors. Were not Adam and Eve also, in a sense, brother and sister, coming as they did from the same parentage?

Phillip and Carol

I was married for the first time, at twenty, to a woman named Carol, who was twenty-two. We both felt we were mature for our age, and our marriage was a way of signaling the world of our eagerness to take on the responsibilities and commitments of adulthood. In retrospect, I see I grossly overestimated my level of maturity and self-awareness: I was only bluffing the role of an adult.

Shortly after my graduation, cashing in our wedding presents for a year abroad, we boarded a Yugoslavian freighter, then the cheapest way to cross the Atlantic. I remember the goatish, chess-playing Yugoslav sailors always trying to get me drunk on slivovitz so that they could make time with Carol. But I had absolute confidence in her loyalty: I married her in part because she seemed so kind, so sweet, so devoted to me. She was also brainy, an anthropology major interested in writing, and pretty, with sandy brown hair, sparkling green eyes, a shy rueful smile, and a curvy figure. At first I underappreciated how beautiful she was. I thought her attractive, certainly, but I was surprised when one of my best friends, on meeting her for the first time, remarked, "Boy, Phillip, she's a piece! You never mentioned that." The sailors made it clear that any man might desire her; but I tended to lose sight of that soon enough because, in the particular dynamic of our marriage, I was treated as the peacock, the visionary, and she as the devotee; I had gotten too spoiled with this picture to alter it.

The freighter touched down in Tangiers, where we spent a fascinating week—Arabic culture carried for us, as Jews, an air of excitement and fear, and a deeper, ur-Semitic tie—before traveling on to Spain, our real destination. During the next ten months, we settled into a nesting routine, wrote and lived on the tightest of budgets. To treat ourselves before going home, we decided to return to Morocco for a month. Spain had proven somewhat disappointing—too much like America— whereas Morocco had seemed genuinely different or, as we say now, Other.

Carol was the perfect traveling companion: inquisitive, good-humored, willing to match me mile for mile. As we walked we would compare our observations, and dissect the characters we met. We liked to think we thought as much alike as two people can; and a good deal of our conversation was dedicated to ensuring that accord. Young couples often need to fantasize that their thoughts and feelings are in harmony, that they hold no secrets from each other—that they are two halves of the same psyche. Perhaps it comes from the anxiety of embarking on a new life together in a threatening world: the "orphans in a storm" syndrome. Two young people somewhat frightened of life, we clung to each other like brother and sister. I've seen many graduate student couples take on that siblingesque quality, gladly sacrificing the sexiness of youth for a more stoop-shouldered, reasonable companionship. At least temporarily: sometimes they wake up five years down the line and decide they've missed out on a wider eros. This is more or less what happened to us. But even after we rebelled against the constrictions of marrying too young, I often thought: If only I'd met Carol when we were both older, we could have been the happiest of couples, going to museums, comparing notes after dinner parties, gratefully making love. . . .

In any event, there we were in Morocco, on our way from Marrakech to the next big city, Casablanca, which would be our last stop before taking the airplane back to New York. We had boarded a bus for a ride that began at dawn and was scheduled to last twelve to fifteen hours. I don't know what Moroccan buses or roads are like now, but in 1965 they were primitive. The bus driver seemed to be new on the job, and each mountain curve he took threatened, it seemed, to plunge us into a ravine below. I was also suffering from a headache and a carsick, nauseous feeling—occasioned by the couscous I had eaten in the marketplace the night before, though Carol seemed to be showing no ill effects. My only consolation was that the bus would be stopping for an hour in a mountain town called Beni-Mellal, roughly midway.

Beni-Mellal was a town that seemed to exist solely to let travelers stretch their legs. No doubt it was also an entrepôt and agricultural center, but what you noticed chiefly on de-boarding were the kids with their hands stretched out, the teenagers offering or threatening to take your bags, the flies, the chewing gum vendors. All this might have struck me as amusing another day; but with the hard-boiled egg I'd gobbled at dawn still squatting on my chest, and with my bowels making ominous pincer moves, I felt the urgent need to sit down and close my eyes. The heat seemed oppressive, and there was no shade in sight. "What's wrong?" Carol asked. I told her I needed a john, and was not sure I was fit to continue. If Beni-Mellal had an inn of some sort, it might be good to spend the night there, and catch the next bus to Casablanca tomorrow.

We were in luck: Beni-Mellal did have an adequate, even pleasant, hotel at the top of the hill, run by ex-colonials. It was one of those oases obstinately more Gallic than Paris, with French sports papers and other periodicals arriving six weeks late. After visiting the w.c., I took a nap, and Carol went out to reconnoiter the town.

An hour later she returned to say that Beni-Mellal was more interesting than it had first appeared. With her anthropologist's training, she was always scrutinizing hill towns on our travels and imagining what sort of study she might do, if she had a grant and a year or two to stay there. This time she had met a man on her walk who told her that that night Beni-Mellal was to host a Moroccan music festival—there would be folk music scattered through the village. "What a pity you feel so rotten," she said. "Maybe you'll recover in a few hours and we can both go out and hear the music, which everyone says is great."

I was sick as a dog. My plans were to stay close to the toilet: if Blind Lemon Jefferson had risen from the grave to sing at the local dance, I would have passed him up. I told Carol it was fine for her to go, if she wanted to. Actually, of course, I wanted her to stay behind and take care of me. I even assumed she would, as she was usually such a good nurse. But she surprised me by accepting my offer. She may have said, "Are you sure?" but it was too late for me to abandon my noble pose, and I did not want to be one of those boorish husbands who chain their wives. In a way, it was a test: I wanted her to *choose* to stay at my side, and could only find out if that was her genuine wish by assuring her it wasn't necessary. Always a mistake to say the opposite of what you mean. So she left.

I began shivering in bed, unable to get warm, and the insides of my stomach swirled until I thought it might be a good idea to vomit, and from that thought ensued the realization that I could not *not* vomit, which I did with my head over the bowl. I felt like a child again, unable to control my involuntary re-flexes. This was followed by a run of diarrhea that lasted for hours. A maid came in to mop up the excess vomit on the floor. She helped me back to my bed, asking, "Where is your wife?" Where indeed.

It was ten at night before I could finally stop running to the bathroom. My mood had shifted by then from self-pity at being abandoned to worrying about Carol: why had she not come home yet? I waited a quarter-hour more, then made my-self get dressed to look for her. Shivering with fever, innards still promising turmoil, I was not in the best shape to go searching. But I had no choice. I had to go out into the Moroccan night, into a strange village I knew not at all, and—protect my wife.

I headed down the hill toward some music issuing from a square white shack. I made up my mind to signal her from the doorway; she would get up, apologizing to her guide, and we would walk home, not without a lecture from me. I opened the door and saw about fifty men sitting in burnouses and embroidered caps, with hashish pipes at their feet. No sign of Carol. I forced my eyes to move row by row over the dark faces, in case I had overlooked her. The eyes that met mine were imperturbably grave, telling me I had no business intruding on their ceremony. The plangent, trancelike, melancholy music, a cousin to Coltrane, appealed to me, but I could not play the concert-goer. I moved on.

In the distance, scattered over the hills, I saw cottages with lights on, and moved toward each. In this way, I backtracked across the town for the next hour, passing the all-night café where truckers sat hunched over stools; the bus stop where poor Moroccan women patiently waited with string-tied parcels; the boarded-up market stalls. Each time I entered a hut I would see men crouched on the floor, listening stolidly to the musicmakers. There were no women. What could Carol have been thinking of?

Around midnight I met a sympathetic-looking young man in a *jelaba*, who asked me (in French) whether I needed help. I told him (in French) I was looking for my wife. She had gone to hear some music. He insisted on accompanying me; and, with that weird, persistent hospitality toward lost strangers one encounters abroad, stuck by my side.

He kept questioning me why my wife was not with me.

"She wanted to hear the music."

"And you were sick? And she left you?" He shook his head. It was incomprehensible to him: proof that the decadent West had no values. Equally incomprehensible to him was that I had entrusted my wife to a man whose last name I didn't even know.

He stopped by his fiancée's house to tell her where he was, and she, a spirited young woman (from what I could make out through her veil), joined us. Though they conversed freely enough, she walked a step or two behind him. I could not have been given a sharper demonstration of the proper respect a woman in that part of the world is expected to show her man. While I was not about to embrace a system that kept women in chador, I admit I felt ashamed of myself for not having been more of a man: it now felt a cowardice on my part to have let Carol take off by herself, when I had wanted her to stay behind with me. Worse, for the sake of appearing liberal, I had let her be subjected to God knows what dangers. I promised God I would never do it again, if only she would materialize at the next corner.

By two in the morning we were ready to try the police, but decided to check back at the hotel one more time. I was over-joyed to learn from the night clerk that my wife had returned. I could not thank the young Moroccan couple enough; they, for their part, were happy that everything had turned out well.

Carol seemed chastened, reluctant to talk. She said that the man and his friend had taken her by truck to the outskirts of town, ostensibly to hear music, and had tried to rape her. She managed to fend them off and make her way back to town. She clearly needed comforting; regrettably, the lecture would have to wait.

We stayed for five days longer in Beni-Mellal, while I re-gained my health. During that time I dragged a little more out of her about the experience: that the men in the truck had been obsessed with American movies—Doris Day in particular; that they craved all they saw in these films, the Frigidaires, the swimming pools; that they had cast her in the Doris Day mold, which made them avid and resentful.

While I took her word for it that she had not been raped—she would have acted more distraught if she had—another part of me lingered on the suspicion that more had happened with these men than she was letting on. She seemed tainted in my eyes, somehow, by the events of that night. How had it happened, I kept brooding, that I had so misjudged her? She had always seemed to me the most dependable, caring woman imaginable: perhaps because she was two years older than I, I had projected onto her a settled, mothering maturity. But she was still a young woman, struggling to sort out her desires, and was there not another, more wayward side of her, resisting the "good wife" role?

Beni-Mellal produced the first fracture of trust between us. In time to come, there would be other infractions, mutual betrayals. I fancied she "owed me one" after Beni-Mellal. How childish, I think now, that I had fastened on her "abandoning" of me, while ignoring for the most part her trauma.

I pondered my own complicity, using the memory to worry feelings of unmanliness that always lie in wait. Had I been too much the brother with her, not the husband? Was I a Francis Macomber, what Hemingway calls "the American boy-man"? Had I, unconsciously, tempted her into neglecting me, to satisfy some atavistic scenario about women-as-betrayers?

All my life, I have been transfixed by the drama of whether the woman I was with would prove trustworthy and caring, or bitchy and unchaste. Many of the women I have sought out since Carol were much less nurturing than she—in fact self-absorbed and fickle. Perhaps it was more important for me to avoid a nurturing solace (with its threat of reawakened incest

taboo) than to swallow the expected bitterness of being poorly
loved. Others may well ask: What exactly do I mean by "nurturing"? What sexist fantasies lie beneath that term? What exi-
gent standards constitute a truly nurturing woman for a
mistrustful man like me? "A woman of valor who can find?"
(Proverbs 31:10)

Freud teaches that every love object is but a surrogate for
the original one and must disappoint because of that. Had I
known then what I know now, I might still be married to
Carol. Abraham and Sarah could forgive each other again and
again for their ambiguous adventures; but perhaps this is the
difference in wisdom between an older and a younger man.
"All things can be replaced," says the Talmud, "except the wife
of one's youth."

---

1. The first episode, in Egypt, occurs before Abram's name has been
   changed to Abraham and Sarai's to Sarah; the second incident, in
   Gerar, takes place after the name change. For the sake of conve-
   nience, I will refer to the couple throughout this essay as Abraham
   and Sarah.

2. The contrasting modern tendency is to downplay his apprehen-
   sions perhaps too much, as when Harold Bloom, in *The Book of J*,
   translated by David Rosenberg, writes that Abraham "oddly fears
   that his wife's beauty will expose him to danger"—the "oddly"
   making him sound borderline paranoid.

3. There is a wonderful commentary in the Babylonian Talmud about
   this, which Francine Klagsbrun quotes in *Voices of Wisdom*: "In the
   Book of Genesis, when God tells Sarah she is to have a son, she
   laughs and says, 'Now that I am withered, am I to have enjoyment—with my husband so old?' When God relates the incident to
   Abraham, He is recorded as saying, 'Why did Sarah laugh, saying,
   "Shall I in truth bear a child, old as I am?"' According to the rabbis,

God deliberately changed Sarah's words in telling them to Abraham so as not to reveal that his wife had complained of his old age. At the school of Rabbi Ishmael it was taught: Great is the cause of peace, seeing that for the sake of peace even the Holy One, blessed be He, deviated from the truth and modified a statement."

The Story of Sarah's Late Pregnancy

Norma Rosen

A few years ago I partici-
pated in a women's Passover seder where each of us was invited
to speak of personal connection to one of three biblical
women: Sarah, Miriam, or Deborah. Deborah, the acclaimed
prophet and judge, was eagerly embraced by most. Miriam,
the ambiguous figure who is sister to Moses and occasional
prophet, alternately praised and punished, was named by a
few. No one chose Sarah.

Until my turn. Sarah's story, so simple on the surface, I
said, was full of richness and complexity, and deserved our
attention.

A woman in the room, known for forthright political views
and broad-brimmed hats, stared while I spoke. Then she pro-
claimed: Sarah was submissive and passive! Sarah was of no interest as a model for modern women! Sarah's behavior was
contemptible!

This approach to reading the Bible struck me speechless. Years later it is no less astonishing, though I've come to see it as the Bible's triumph over reductive reading. That woman in the room who had excoriated Sarah (and me for choosing her), who was so passionately bound to politico-feminist matters, not Bible tradition or text, was in fact engaging with biblical language and episodes where I have no doubt she encountered, despite resistance, ideas and emotions deep enough to drown the politics of any day.

The Bible writer invents (or transforms) stories, invents (or transforms) God, so as to make us long for God again. Makes us long for God though we've said we see through this child's play, though religion is only quotation for us now, and at most we aspire to brush against the consciousness of our ancestors who once believed all that. In this experience we resemble Sarah. Sarah has reconciled herself to doing without. Then Sarah is given what she no longer wants and is forced to discover feeling for what she's been given. Reattached to life in old age, Sarah is challenged to find passion again.

But now we are too far ahead of the necessary first question. The necessary first question is: *Who* is Sarah?

Sarah is introduced to us as a woman on whom God is playing a joke. She is ninety years old when she and Abraham, their marriage well marinated by time, hear the annunciation by God in Genesis 18:10 that she will bear a son.

Sarah laughed within herself, saying:

> After I am waxed old shall I have pleasure, my lord being old also? And the Lord said unto Abraham . . . Is anything too hard for the Lord?

Sarah laughed. If she hadn't laughed she might have burst out with the rage that a stressed laugh masks.

Who *is* Sarah? What does Sarah *want*? Did she *ever* express longing for a child?

If Sarah were being cast in a play, we might imagine a director giving the actress a feel for the role:

"Come up on stage, Sarah. Let's see who you are. You're a beautiful woman. Or used to be, before you got old. Not intelligent, we don't know that. Not scheming like Rebekah or devious like Rachel or any of those matriarchs. Just beautiful. And now you're old. Greta Garbo after the fall of the chin-line! Gloria Swanson in *Sunset Boulevard!* You're old, you hate it, you used to be beautiful, and now on top of everything you're pregnant! Do you want a child? Who knows? Maybe—once. Now you're so old you're being reminded it takes a miracle to make you conceive. *You're* not having the child, *God* is having the child! You're a surrogate womb, okay? And you don't like it! On top of that, you might have prophetic powers, too, like some of those other matriarchs, and you foresee tragedy!

"So you laugh. You're not a walk-on, you're a laugh-on. What kind of laugh—happy? Not a chance! A '*now* you tell me?' laugh. A 'you think I *want* this?' laugh. Sarah can't afford straight-out rage. This is a *zapper* God. Her laugh needs some of everything. You'll have to work on it."

There is no text for Sarah, pre-annunciation, except an early enforced harem period. Also a joke. A spell of harem-scarem to save Abraham's hide. Genesis 12:11–15 introduces Sarah in her sexual role:

> And it came to pass, when he was come near to enter into Egypt, that he said unto Sarai his wife, Behold now, I know that thou art a fair woman to look upon: therefore it shall come to pass when the Egyptians shall see thee, that they will save thee alive. Say, I pray thee, thou art my sister: That it may be well with me for thy sake; and my soul shall live because of thee . . . and the woman was taken into Pharaoh's house.

Can we hear from the audience? What do we think of Sarah having to sleep with Pharaoh to save her husband?

—*Disgusting!*
—*Husband cowardly!*
—*Wife submissive!*

When next we see Sarah her sexual role is finished. Sarah is old. *Then* the announcement is made: Sarah will give birth! Abraham falls on his face laughing (Genesis 17:17), but God doesn't comment. Sarah, who laughs behind the tent flap like a Japanese lady behind her fan, is at once challenged by God (Genesis 18:13–15):

> Wherefore did Sarah laugh . . . ? Then Sarah denied, saying, I laughed not; for she was afraid. And he said, Nay; but thou didst laugh.

As predicted, Sarah bears a son, Isaac.
Can we hear from the audience? What do we think of Sarah giving birth at age ninety anyway?
—*Disgusting!*
—*Right on! Don't talk to me about biological clocks ticking!*

Sarah becomes so much a mother that she banishes Ishmael, son of Abraham by Hagar, Abraham's concubine. No one is to stand in the light of Sarah's precious boy. In giving birth to Isaac, Sarah gives birth to herself. Here she resembles the aged Naomi in the Book of Ruth. The death of Naomi's sons and husband have robbed her of the will to live. Only by attachment to her daughter-in-law, Ruth, is Naomi reawakened to passionate concern. But when Sarah's emotional life is at full fever-heat and focused on Isaac, he is snatched away by the power behind the voice that thrust a son upon her in the first place.

God toys with Sarah in decreeing that a son be born to her, and toys with her again in decreeing that son's death. The treasure foisted on Sarah (without her having expressed any desire for it) is stolen from her by the *Akedah,* the binding and near-sacrifice of Isaac by his father. Now Sarah is no longer like

Naomi. She becomes more Job than Job, since for her there can be no fobbing off with new family. Jewish legend tells us that Sarah dies believing that her husband killed her son or, at the very least, was *willing* to kill him.

Like Naomi? Like Job? Who is Sarah? If we link her to another woman of the Bible—Rachel, wife of Sarah's grandson Jacob—we see another facet.

Rachel steals her father's idols to take with her when she leaves home with Jacob. Her father discovers their loss and challenges the departing party. Jacob swears death to the thief, who is never found. Rachel, the culprit, has hidden the idols in her saddle pack. She sits on them and does not get up when the search is on. Then she lies to her father in Genesis 31:35:

> Let it not displease my lord that I cannot rise up before thee; for the custom of women is upon me.

In one sentence Rachel sounds an irony that manages to conflate her own need, male abhorrence of menstrual blood, and the female's free fall from father to husband. Rachel takes away something of home—idols, despised by the Hebrews. Jacob is grandson of Abraham, smasher of *his* father's idols, according to another Jewish legend. Rachel wants them—why? To save her father from further sinning? To keep their idol magic near her in a strange new home? Perhaps they are female idols, goddesses, and Rachel, who says that she is menstruating, may be trying to insure goddess-induced fertility.

Some sources believe that the character of Sarah derives from fertility goddesses in ancient religions supplanted by, or incorporated into, Judaism. For early rabbinic interpreters, the fecundity of barren Sarah symbolized the rebirth of Israel. The Kabbalists, intuiting other meanings, carried symbolism deeper into the past. They modulated the *Shekhina*, God's Presence, into the female aspect of godhead whose passionate coupling with the male aspect creates the oneness of God. Raphael Patai's

The Hebrew Goddess brings us the startling declaration of the thirteenth-century Kabbalist, Joseph ben Abraham Gikatilla: "In the days of Abraham the *Shekhina* was called Sarah." Moreover the legend that Sarah, giving birth, had enough milk in her breasts to suckle a countryside of babies (recounted by Bialik and Ravnitzky in *The Book of Legends from Talmud and Midrash*) recalls the many-breasted mother goddess of the ancient world. Without putting too fine a point on matters, we can reflect on Sarah's relationship to these figures of antiquity and arrive at a rich palimpsest, a pentimento of versions of proliferating worship impulse, trace of suppressed cults, carried by Sarah. (At the last trump perhaps they will all be overlaid one upon the other, and the phrases of one will peer through the pages of another, refracting into one grand pattern of story, with nothing more ever needing to be said.)

Meanwhile, I find a nice symmetry in the idea of Rachel carrying Sarah to her new home, the goddess mother-in-law one generation removed. Sarah's son Isaac marries Rebekah, who reminds Isaac of his dead mother.

> And Isaac brought her into his mother Sarah's tent, and he took Rebekah, and she became his wife; and he loved her; and Isaac was comforted after his mother's death (Genesis 24:67).

Rebekah in turn sends their son Jacob far away to seek a wife. Jacob, who never sees his mother again, bursts into tears at first sight of Rachel, his beloved. Two motherless boys, one generation apart, both descended from the beautiful Sarah, who may or may not have wanted a child in the first place, both locked into mother-love, then into wife-love, for life.

Still—setting out anew, one wants something from home. It can only be stolen, a piece ripped away, out of context. You can't take the whole thing. Rarely do you want it all, only what you can use—a reminder, if nothing else, of the magic that makes you who you are. Rachel's willingness to accept Leah in

Jacob's bed for the first seven years may indicate a certain ambivalence on her part concerning marriage. The romance of the rabbis assumes her as crushed by the delay as love-smitten Jacob. But Rachel may have welcomed the wait! Those idols she steals may be to her not only the grown-up woman's fertility-goddess but the dolls and toys of home, teddy bears of childhood. Rachel dies young, in childbirth, perhaps still a child herself, perhaps still mourning home.

But Sarah—strong, persistent Sarah—is never in doubt.

—Is it necessary for me to lie with this desert despot? Then let me do it!

—My handmaid conceived in my place. Now I must reclaim that place!

And ultimately, when Sarah's son Isaac is born, Sarah never equivocates. Against Abraham's protest, she throws out the rival son and his mother. They're to have a nation of their own, but Sarah probably doesn't know that. Might Ishmael and Hagar die in the desert? That's no concern of Sarah's.

Can we hear from the audience? What do we think of Sarah ejecting Hagar and Ishmael from the house?

—*Disgusting!*

—*Husband cowardly!*

—*Wife finally not submissive!*

Through our longings we are snared into life. We wanted what we couldn't have, we did the grown-up thing and suppressed the desire, made do with something else, now it comes back! Not the desire—no. The *goal* of desire, of the desire that no longer fires us. Now we have to work up desire again to fit the goal we wanted once, but no longer. To do that we have to pick away the years scab by scab, getting down to the old wound—I want! I can't have! But I *want!* But I *can't have!*

Now the truth of the old saying comes home—what you wish for in youth you'll get in old age. Written on the world are the reprieves that came too late. The reprieve of the ram that saves Isaac's life comes too late for Sarah, of whom one legend says she died hearing only of Abraham's attempt to kill Isaac, and not of God's intervention.

Sarah could not live with the thought of Isaac's death. Could not live life now without Isaac, or change her conception of herself or her life. The irony of Sarah's death is that Isaac's death, the insupportable agony, does not occur. That's a happy ending to the tale, if you don't think about Sarah's death or imagine her state of mind at the command to slaughter Isaac. If Sarah could have said, "Very well, my beloved son will be taken from me, I will again live with nothing," Sarah could have had everything. But she would no longer have been Sarah. If she had known that Isaac was spared, could she have lived? But how would she have lived with the knowledge of Abraham's willingness to kill Isaac? That, too, would have meant that she could no longer be Sarah.

Do we at last know who Sarah is?

Only the *Akedah*, the binding and near sacrifice of Isaac by his father, undoes Sarah. She contributes nothing to that Bible episode except to die when it is over. (The omission of any response by Sarah to this section of Bible text seems so entirely unlike her that I was compelled to imagine an extension of Sarah's story in my book, *Unbinding the Mothers* [Jewish Publication Society, 1996]. There, Sarah decisively pursues Abraham and Isaac up Mount Moriah to put a stop to the shameful goings-on, and initiates a dispute with God near the slaughter site, all for the sake of the once unwanted son for whom she now longs with all her soul.)

We who are formed by the Western world lean a lavish amount of our mental, emotional, and intellectual condition on episodes in the lives of biblical figures. The attention and (occasional) devotion we give these biblical folk bear some relation to our perception of boundaries of the human condition.

As if someone said: "Take all the sad human limitations and turn them on their heads! Don't we know people who die of disease and hardship by age forty? Then let's say that once they lived to be hundreds of years old. And don't we know that women age and wear in this life, their fertility giving out before wrinkles are well in, menopause following first menses before you have time to utter, 'Let it not displease my lord that I cannot rise before thee'? Then let's say that once there was a woman named Sarah who could give birth at age ninety. And that she had enough milk in her breasts to feed her child and the whole countryside of children as well! And since we human beings have to bewail our fate, though we've no one to cry to once Mother is gone, let's write that there exists a Power to whom we address our needs, and that once in a while this Power gives an ear and an answer! Let's write a world in which not chaos and evil and random events reeking of unjust reward and punishment prevail, but where justice and righteousness are the norm, and a Power oversees it all. Let's write ourselves a world with meaning to it!"

Sarah's struggle expresses a theme of importance in my own work as well as in much American life and literature. Starting far back. Having to overcome obstacles even to get to a starting place. Starting from too far back to achieve what is desired, yet with the burning longing to achieve it, has been a theme as true of protagonists in my other novels as it was of real-life Anzia Yezierska and John Dewey, on whom I based *John and Anzia: An American Romance.* That achieving darkens under the shadow side: the knowledge that goals, by the time of our achieving them, have utterly altered. The goal has altered, you have altered, the times have altered. Nothing means what you thought it would mean. Now you must consciously alter yourself—CHANGE OR DIE! Must create within yourself whatever will make the goal recognizable to your inner being once more, will infuse old age with youth and death with life. Some Talmudic rabbis agreed (astonishingly, for a life-affirming religion!) that it is better not to be born. Still, given the given of birth, the question—implicit with gratitude for what *is*—profoundly resonates for us: "How is it that there is not *nothing?*"

The enforced birth of longing that occurred in Sarah with Isaac's birth becomes the means through which Sarah herself is born.

This is the journey the human narrative was made for. Not linear—circular. In my beginning is my end, and in the closing of that circle, as being abrogates becoming, is the cessation of all story, all longing. Only there do we win our freedom, but it is not the freedom of this world.

When that director calls Sarah up to the stage to explain her role, he is saying, "Your turn to be born as a character in God's play. Your turn to come on-stage as a character in this play someone is writing and saying that God is writing it."

> *The writer said:*
> *Let there be a world of truth and meaning.*
> *The writer called the world:*
> *Good!*
> *Then the writer said:*
> *Let there be a listening, answering Power.*
> *The writer called the Power:*
> *God!*

And the strange thing—the very strangely moving, mysterious, haunting, and enduring thing, as if the writer had listened in on some secret code, had stumbled on or intuited supernal knowledge, had, through Sarah, peered into the very palm of heaven—is that on some days the words of the writer appear to us to be true.

The Story of
Sarah and Hagar

Lore Segal

Coming round by the threshing floor, one of the oxen tripped. The ark, which King David was moving into new-conquered Jerusalem, must have looked to be toppling for the young man, Uzza, who walked beside it, reached his hand to steady the sacred object. And God "broke" him, says the Hebrew. Uzza died on the spot.

Even an unbeliever like me faintly shudders at the approach to the Bible's awe-ful domain, and without the scholar's passport. Shouldn't someone stop me at the gates? Do I know how to read stories written, the believer says, at God's dictation and about events that happened three millennia ago in such a distant climate, such an alien geography?

Why try? The Bible's stories are more interesting than my own dreams, and because the manner of their telling (like the telling of myth and myth's little sister, fairy tale) is the manner in which I would wish to tell my stories.

———————

Imagine that the object of my impertinence isn't God's first family but a work of my own day—a Brancusi sculpture. It's called *Beginning of the World,* a polished bronze. It reflects me, radically distorted, along with the viewers who stand behind me, and several other works by the same artist, and our environment—a wall, a corner of the ceiling, lights. The *Beginning of the World* is at once featureless and complex. Where the indication of a line interrupts the perfection of the almost egg-shape, the plane alters and reflects a different perspective of walls, works, and viewers. Unless the lights by which I view the object are turned off, I am unable to reflect myself away from the *Beginning of the World* in which I am a helpless participant.

Not all arts are as reflexive as a Brancusi, or a biblical narrative. Erich Auerbach's *Mimesis* suggests that the Bible's very absence of feature forces our reflection upon it. We are unable *not* to participate in stories so bare of the details we need in order to see anything. Like the medieval Midrash (or old Judaic commentary), our modern speculation rushes to fill in the narrative gaps, account for improbabilities, and harmonize the contradictions. We worry when our ancient parents don't behave the way we think the Bible taught us that they ought.

The Bible stories seldom say what someone looks like. If Abraham has a beard, I grew it on him. Out here, in my world, fathers are overweight or wizened, but I have imposed upon the first patriarch a vigorous (bearded) old age learned from Michelangelo. It's not till Genesis 18:11–12, where Sarah sadly laughs at her old husband's impotence, that Abraham's skin sags under his chin.

The Bible's rare physical details are not visual aids to the mind's eye but conventions, or elements of plot. If Sarah is

beautiful, it is with the generic beauty of fairy-tale queens. Her
name means princess. Painters use their neighbor's wife for
models because our visual imagination won't supply Sara
with a particular length of nose, or the color of the eye, or the
arrangement of her hair. Nor does the text talk about Sarah's
beauty until the plot sends the old couple down to Egypt to escape one of those Canaanite famines. Here's where Abraham
says to her:

> Look, I know what a beautiful woman you are. When the Egyp-
> tians see you they will . . . kill me and will let you live.[1]

The Midrash says Abraham hadn't known Sarah to be beautiful hitherto because she, in her modesty, went veiled, but that in
crossing the river her face had become exposed.[2] How is it, the
rabbis wonder, that an old woman was still so attractive that
kings desired her? They explain that she had regained her youth.[3]

I want to explain that the story makes Sarah beautiful for its
self-preservation: If she wasn't beautiful, and didn't attract
kings, there *is* no story.

Abraham goes on:

> Say you are my sister, and then things will go well with me be-
> cause of you.

It goes very well for him. The Lord sends His plague to punish Pharaoh's court for Sarah's presence in it. Pharaoh sends
for Abraham and says:

> What have you done to me! Here! Here is your wife. Take her
> and go away.

Both in this, and the cognate story that sends the couple to
Gerar, Abraham comes away a richer man.

The moral troubles me, and seems to have troubled the rabbis. I checked out their commentaries on the subject in the notes
of the Soncino Chumash. They want to prove that foreigners are

evil: One called Sforno says Egypt was notorious for its low standard of morality; they were a dark-skinned, ugly people, says Nachmanides.[4] The rabbis and I have different agendas: They want to exculpate the bad behavior of our own. I like pointing it out: To me it looks as if the foreigners behaved rather better than our father Abraham.

How, in the absence of the story's guidance, does the mind's eye envisage Abraham's person when he is in God's presence? I see the old man's (bearded) chin raised toward the top left corner where I have imagined God off the page in order to resist the temptation to imagine *Him*. Sometimes the story says that Abraham stood, and sometimes that he prostrated himself, whereupon he lies down, in my mind's eye, on his stomach. And there are the times when the Lord has had enough of conversation with the human and rises up and away.

Behind our two actors—the old man and his God (whose beard I am at pains to unimagine)—the background is as bare as the stage of the Globe Theater. What do we put into that space? Is Haran a city? A landscape of horizontal distances or mountains? We could look in the atlas, but the imagination is not prone to research. Nor are we able to leave the scene empty: We don't know what "empty" looks like.

I think I see a vastness empty of the populations with which God repeatedly commands man and beast to fill up the new world, and which will be as the grains of sand, too many to count.

The Bible's manner of storytelling fulfills its own commandment against image-making. Curious that God forbids the making of idols out of the visual image to bow ourselves down in front of. He must know we make idols out of anything— stories, phrases, names, ideas.

It is not only, or chiefly, the visual detail that biblical narrative leaves to speculation. Not only does the Bible not draw us pictures, it does not often tell what characters are thinking or feeling. We are left to deduce the characters' reactions from
their actions and their conversation. Nor does the Bible explain anything it means.

What does the story say about Abraham and Sarah? In what sense are they "characters"? We know not to look for them in history. Do they have personalities such as we expect to find in novels? Do they exhibit characteristic behaviors with the occasional contradictions we observe in our neighbor? Are they as essentially mysterious as we are to ourselves?

Of Abraham we know he is obedient. He, who will question God's idea of justice in the matter of Sodom and Gomorrah, obeys without question the featureless, as-yet-nameless God, who commands him to leave country, kindred, and his father's house. Abraham takes his wife, his nephew, and his substance in cattle and servants, and emigrates westward to a future consisting of a command and a promise.

Every few pages Abram will raise his chin to receive a reiteration of this promise. It becomes located in geography:

> Look north and south and east and west. All the land that you
> can see I will give to you and your children for ever.

The promise becomes legalized by covenant and attaches to itself a set of phrases: Abraham will be the father of multitudes; he will bring forth kings; his children's children will rule this land of Canaan; they will be blessed; they will be a blessing to the nations.

When the Lord foretells the centuries of ill usage by the native populations among whom the children will reside, Abraham knows a black night of the soul. Does he foresee the four hundred years of slavery? Does he fore-suffer the Holocaust?

That the promise of Canaan can fulfill itself only after the expulsion from it of a whole list of the resident populations is an anachronistic problem for this modern reader: It appears not to have discomfited the Lord, nor worried Abraham.

———————————

What does worry Abraham is that he, destined to father multitudes, continues childless. "What good is anything that you give me?" Abraham still hopefully urges the Lord. "I have no children. My chief servant will inherit everything I own."

Servants are an interesting element in the Abraham story: First they share in their master's circumcision. Then, if it isn't Abraham's chief servant who will, by default, inherit God's promise, it looks for a time as if it will have to be Ishmael, Abraham's son by the servant Hagar. Is Abraham no longer quite so sanguine—is his urgency more oblique when he begs the Lord: "If you will only let my son Ishmael live in Your favor!" The Lord reiterates: "Sarah will have a son." Abraham gets points for trusting this more and more implausible promise, and the chief servant, so far from inheriting his master's future, will become the pious instrument in procuring for the true son, Isaac, the true wife from the family back in Haran.

Why does Abraham's God tease His devoted and obedient servant and prevent Sarah from getting on with His own plan for her to carry the chosen seed? Why does He make them wait and wait till Abraham is impotent and Sarah postmenopausal?

The Lord creates opportunities to broadcast his powers.

> Don't you understand that I could stretch out My hand and wipe you and your people off the face of the earth?

He says to Pharaoh before sending the plague of thunder and hail upon him and continues:

I have preserved you in order to show you the greatness of My
might, and to make My name known upon the earth.

Sarah, not as a good believer as her husband, has to laugh
when she overhears the divine promise of the son to be born
to her. God says,

> Why does Sarah laugh and say, How shall I, who am past child
> bearing, have a child? Is there anything so wonderful the Lord
> cannot make it happen? Sarah will bear a son.

"I didn't laugh!" lies the scared Sarah. It is possible to read
the Hebrew to mean that it is Abraham to whom she says this,
but it also gives me room to imagine it is the Lord who answers, "Yes, you did, you laughed."

I think that like ourselves (who are made in His image) the
Lord likes a good story. Observe some of His narrative strategies: When Sarah tells Abraham she wants Hagar out of the
house, God tells him,

> Do not grieve for the boy or for the woman. Do what Sarah
> says. And Abraham rose early in the morning and took bread
> and a flask of water and he put it and the child on Hagar's
> shoulders and sent them away.

Now by this time the child that Abraham puts on Hagar's
shoulder is a strapping thirteen-year-old. Has the story failed
to check its own arithmetic? I think the story cares nothing
about the arithmetic. It cares about Abraham's grief, and it
feels more grievous to send a baby to die of thirst in the desert
than a teenager.

Classic narrative assigns the protagonist a desire that it is the
business of the plot to keep withholding. It might be a treasure;

it might be love and marriage or, as in the story of Abraham and Sarah, the promised child, who will father the children, who will inherit the promise. The plot compounds the difficulties into a virtual impossibility, which it's the job of the denouement to finally and delightfully reverse.

It is this long withholding of the child that will later function to enhance Abraham's phenomenal obedience. Abraham, who sacrificed his father to go to a land of which he knew only that God would show it to him, proves himself willing literally to sacrifice this urgently desired, long denied, miraculously begotten boy born to his old age, circumcised into the covenant, weaned, and grown, on the mountain that God says He will show him. Why does God remind the father that this boy whom He is telling him to butcher and burn is the one he loves? Why does He call Isaac his father's "only" son, when God knows Abraham has another boy, Ishmael, except to turn the emotional screw? This in a narrative whose surface appears so cool, so very spare.

The Lord has availed Himself of the "type story" of the barren wife.

The Bible's childless women grieve over their deprivation, envy their fruitful sisters, fret that they fail their husbands, and fail God's first commandment to man and beast to multiply and populate the new and empty earth.

Ancients and moderns both seem to be commenting on life's sheer cussedness—call it Murphy's, call it God's law: In fairy tales it's the poor women who always bear more children than they can feed; the rich remain childless. In the Bible the unloved wife is fruitful; it's the loved one who is barren.

For twice seven years Jacob labors willingly for love of Rachel, whom the Lord makes barren. But seeing "that Leah

was not beloved, He opened her womb." In the Book of Judges,
it's Peninnah who bears Elkanah children; barren Hannah is
the one he feeds tidbits from the table.

The women know it is the Lord who balks them, but take it
out on their men. As Rachel says to Jacob,

> Give me children, or I shall die. Jacob became angry too and
> said, Do I stand in God's place? Is it I who deny you children?
> Rachel said, Take my maid Bilhah, go in and lie with her and she
> shall bear you a son on my lap, and I shall rear him as my own.

We know that in the ancient Middle East surrogacy was the
cultural norm, as it may become in the modern West. Sarah
says to Abraham,

> I cannot have children. Why don't you go in and lie with my
> slave Hagar? Maybe I can get a son by her.

The Bible's stories happen to human beings. God uses their
faith and He uses their faithlessness to accomplish His ends.
Joseph tells his brothers it was in God's plan for them to sell
him into Egypt, by which means He managed the region's
seven-year famine, kept Israel's family from starvation, and
got them moved down to Egypt for their four-hundred-year
enslavement.

Are we justified in feeling we understand the human angles?
Aren't we practiced in reading sexual triangles—the man and
his two or more women?

Take poor Leah—the older sister whom her father, the cheat
Laban, palmed off on his nephew, the cheat Jacob, to bond him
to a second seven years of labor in order to get his love, Rachel.
Leah is the sort who can't live without hoping:

> Leah conceived and bore a son and called him Reuben and said,
> The name means the Lord sees my unhappiness. Now my hus-
> band will love me! And she conceived again and bore a son and

called him Simeon and said, it means the Lord hears that I am
still unloved, therefore he has given me another son. She conceived again . . . and said, This time my husband will become attached to him for I have borne him three sons! And she called
the child Levi, which means attached. She . . . bore a fourth son
and said, I shall praise the Lord and keep hoping and named the
boy Judah, meaning praise.

And we understand Peninnah when she takes it out on Hannah, when she provokes her, makes her cry and lose her ap-
petite. But what sort of girl do we imagine Hagar to have been?
Beautiful? Young? Was it a native meanness in her that made
her kick the other woman where she knew her to be sore? Was
it the primitive triumph of pregnancy?

I think the Egyptian slave must have grabbed at the opportunity for once to take it out on the mistress who ordered her
into the master's bed. Why would she not have hated her Hebrew overlords the way the Hebrews would come to hate the
Egyptians?

The rabbis are not as interested as I am in quarrels and family feelings. An anonymous medieval commentator writes, "As
dutiful children, let us cover the nakedness of our fathers with
the cloak of a favorable interpretation,"[5] and the favorable interpretation wants to prove our fathers—and our mothers,
too—to be in the right, even if it means proving the Bible story
in need of correction or amplification. Rashi says Hagar was
Pharaoh's daughter, and when she saw the miracles wrought
on behalf of Abraham and Sarah, she said, I would rather be a
servant in their house than a mistress in my own.[6] Sforno says
that when God tells Hagar to return to her mistress, He is saying, "Consider *whence camest thou,* from a holy place and a
righteous house; *and whither goest thou,* to an unclean land
and a place of sinful people."[7]

As a good universalist I'm committed to empathize with all
parties. If I understand Hagar's brief, cruel triumph, I must
also feel for Sarah's unhappy spite. "This is an insult to me and
it is your fault!" she cries to Abraham, who is only doing what
she told him. We can feel his anxiety to appease her.

The Bible's men obey their women when it comes to decisions about the children. With the exception of Abraham,
whom God tells what to call Isaac, it is the woman's part to
name the children. We have seen Leah use her boys' names au-
tobiographically. Jacob lets the sisters, Leah and Rachel, barter
for access to his bed.

Again, it is Hannah who decides to dedicate Samuel to the
Lord's service. Elkanah says, "Do what you think best," in the
same tone of voice in which Abraham tells Sarah: "[Hagar] is
your slave. Do what you think is right."

But what Sarah thinks right in regard to Hagar and the boy
Ishmael is murder.

> Sarah looked at Ishmael, the son whom Hagar, her Egyptian
> slave, had borne Abraham, and the boy was laughing and play-
> ing and Sarah said to Abraham, Get rid of the woman and her
> son. A slave's son shall never share my son's inheritance.

Compare the Grimms' stepmother in "The Juniper Tree":

> Now when the woman looked at her daughter she loved her so
> but looking at the little boy cut her to the heart. It seemed that
> wherever he was standing, he was always in her way and then
> she kept wondering how to get the whole fortune just for her
> daughter, and the evil one got into her so that she began to hate
> the little boy and she would push him around from one corner
> to the other so that there was no quiet place where he could be.

The Grimms' stepmother severs the little boy's head from
his shoulders and cooks him in a stew. The biblical Sarah has
Abraham send mother and child into the waterless desert.

Sforno sees Sarah's first harshness as an appropriate reminder to Hagar of her subordinate position.[8] The prejudice seems not to be against slavery, only against being the slaves. I choose to think the Lord conveyed a two-part message to the runaway: One is "Go back. Put yourself in your mistress's hand"—that is to say, fit yourself into the chain of obedience that slaves owe their masters and masters owe their God. The other is,

> Know that you will bear a son. Your son will be a wild ass of a man. . . . He and his brothers will be enemies. . . . Know also that the Lord will so multiply your children and your children's children, they will be too many to count.

God is saying, You shall have the means of revenge.

As for Abraham's obedience to his wife's wishes, Rashi has his favorable interpretation: Abraham listened to the Holy Spirit within Sarah. Nachmanides is concerned with Abraham's sexual purity: Abraham thought Sarah was right, and for that reason complied with her wish. It was not that he wanted to consort with another woman.[9] But we agree, Nachmanides and I, that something's amiss in that ancient household. Nachmanides seems sorry to have to say Sarah sinned in afflicting Hagar and Abraham sinned in permitting her. That is why God allowed Hagar's descendants to persecute and afflict Abraham and Sarah's descendants.[10]

Since I am not covenanted to the favorable interpretation, I understand the story to be in preparation not only for the Israelites' future enemies but the permission to condemn them: Ishmael fathers the Ishmaelites, as Ham begot the Canaanites, and Lot's two daughters the Ammonites and Moabites. Our enemies are born bad guys—the children, respectively, of a slave, of a father's curse, of two daughters' incest.

I count it a blessing that none of these speculations, additions, distortions, the effects of our politics and prejudice—that neither my malice nor the rabbis' piety—adhere to our original. If you could number the stars, you could count the painters who have given particularity to Adam and Eve's nakedness, have corkscrewed the snake around the apple tree, and specified the background with lushest vegetation. Yet when you return to the scene, isn't it once again wonderfully bare?

When I pass from the room that houses the *Beginning of the World,* I take my reflections away with me. Already the Brancusi has forgotten me—awaiting the next viewer? It does not wait. It does not do anything, though if you pass there it will return your image to your own observation.

---

1. Bible quotations from *The Book of Adam to Moses,* translated by Lore Segal (New York: Knopf, 1987).

2. The Soncino Chumash, p. 62.

3. Soncino Chumash, p. 99.

4. Soncino Chumash, p. 62.

5. My source for this quotation is my colleague Lisa Kiser, who comments that the anonymous author "characteristically captures the medieval desire to save the biblical past via strenuous revisioning of it."

6. Soncino Chumash, p. 75.

7. Soncino Chumash, p. 76.

8. Soncino Chumash, p. 76.

9. Soncino Chumash, p. 75.

10. Soncino Chumash, p. 76.

The Story of Isaac's Sacrifice

Geoffrey Hartman

I have always been intrigued by my wish to know as much as possible. Did that wish belong to me, was it "my" wish? It felt more like a drive, something I could do nothing about, especially when young. Later I suspected this drive was a defense: the desire to know was related, I thought, to being prepared; I would not be caught off guard but would be perpetually conscious, aware, on the *qui vive.* This state of vigilance, this desire not to sleep, was far from the anxiety that I eventually associated with it. My earlier, more pristine condition should be described as wakefulness rather than watchfulness: I was Adam as he pictured himself in Milton's *Paradise Lost,* laid at birth "soft on the flow'ry herb" and, no sooner born, like an animal still semiblind, instinctively exploring the world with new senses and thought.

What I will have to say about the *Akedah,* the binding and near-sacrifice of Isaac by his father, includes the later period, when everything began to be accompanied by second thoughts, and questions arose about limits of the knowable. Surely there also existed a traumatic knowledge: was I about to cross a dangerous threshold, would full consciousness lead to terror and feelings of powerlessness? Yet the story of the near-sacrifice of Isaac held no surprise. Mostly because my earlier desire to know was based on trust—that knowledge is good, of the good. Even if "of good and evil," the evil had no power over me: I had no human fears. Hence this Bible story had to have a happy ending. Though attracted to the darkness, my later and more baffled knowledge-drive superimposed itself on basic trust as in a palimpsest. Returning to the text, I realized that as soon as creation had occurred, the major theme of the Book of Genesis became *survival.*

When the Bible said God saw that what he created was good, the phrase now seemed to imply a judgment, and raised the possibility that between the intention and the act, between the fiat and its immediate, obedient consequence, a shadow might have fallen, and God might have had to pronounce the world . . . evil. That glimmer of a Manichaean thought is "limited" by Scripture, by a technique similar to the one that forbids us to inquire about God before the Beginning—we are steered away from such curious questions by the magisterial opening, "In the beginning God created heaven and earth." Any evil found in the creation comes, we are soon specifically told, from man's heart. Human survival is threatened not because God is flawed or has two natures but because an insubordinate mankind tries to rise up and claim divine status.

The playground of Midrash extends the theme of survival into the period before creation. There are many legends in which the angels warn God about the very idea of man as a species: they do not want him to be created. (In the beginning was envy.) Thus it is touch-and-go with the human race from the start. There is the temptation in Eden, there is Cain, there is the Flood, there is Babel; and the struggle to survive continues after God's Covenant with Abraham. We learn that it is necessary to survive God as well as mankind. "Thou hast

struggled with God and men and prevailed" (Genesis 32:29)—
the name Israel is dearly earned. Danger comes from God, not
only from mankind.

Scripture seeks life more than knowledge, or knowledge that
contributes to life. It condenses that knowledge into legends as
well as laws. Bible stories are at once fascinating and baffling.
We enjoy them, and are not tempted to trade them in for their
legal or practical wisdom. At most, they teach us through storytelling to delight in law itself.[1] But even in this regard Genesis
22 seems exceptional. The episode does not imply an authoritative rule of conduct that can be learnt, though it could be
said to exemplify ethical readiness, Abraham's exemplary *hineni* ("Here I am"), his listening to the call, and so, by extension, our own *hineni*: "And it came to pass after these things,
that God tried Abraham, and said to him: 'Abraham.' And he
said: 'Here I am.'" Yet the call is one thing, what it demands another. Is the mother justified who, as reported in the papers,
drowned her baby and claimed, "God asked me to"?

Christian interpretation, in which the *Akedah* prefigures
God's sacrifice of his own son, is other-than-ethical, or shows,
by a later miracle, the very difference between divine and
human. There is certainly no known ritual that is explained by
the *Akedah*. To think that this action, as represented, had daily
significance or disclosed something imitable about God would
take us into the disorder of mystery. There is no hint here, or
for that matter in most Genesis stories, that we stand before a
secret.

If we insist on searching for a religious or cultural practice
this story comments on or seeks to reform, it would have to be
human sacrifice. Scholars are generally agreed, however, that
the displacement of human by animal sacrifice was not a burning issue that needed legislation. The focus, in any case, is on

child sacrifice; children were at risk then as now, both in ordinary circumstances (exposure) and in crisis circumstances that seemed to require such sacrifices (to Moloch, compare Agamemnon's sacrifice of Iphigenia). Here there is no indication of a crisis. On the contrary, Abraham had been given a promise by God: the reiterated "blessing" of Genesis 12, the assurance that his offspring would grow into a nation.

The placement of the *Akedah* story in the Bible makes it, if anything, more perplexing. In Genesis 21, the previous chapter, a threat against the child comes from within the household: Sarah exiles—in fact, exposes—Ishmael. Yet the God who succored Ishmael *then* endangers Isaac *now*. This is confusing; one might have expected a rebellious Isaac, say, who incurs the wrath of a father ready to slay him, and a God who intervenes to stay the father's hand. It is clear from the way Abraham is made to argue with God in the Sodom and Gomorrah episode, where he succeeds in modifying God's wrath, that the rule of *pikuah nefesh* (preservation of life) is already active. Yet in the *Akedah* there is no arguing—hardly an exchange of words. After Abraham's "Here I am" (22:1) there is only a second and third "Here I am" (22:7 and 11).

Though we are always aware of words as speech acts in the Bible—what is uttered remains close to the performative, close to a world in which an oral law prevails and words are bonds—not only is the narrative of Genesis 22 especially sparse but so is direct speech. When it occurs, it breaks a brooding silence. "Brooding" already says too much, however; the very absence of epithets in the story provokes them in our re-creative attempts to understand it. For the same reason, it seems impossible to read the story without adding some psychological decoration. Even Erich Auerbach, in *Mimesis,* succumbs at one point: "Bitter is the dawn, in which Abraham saddles his ass, summons his servants and his son Isaac and prepares to set out."[2] Combined with an iconic minimalism, that is, with

the strict subordination of all visual detail to a portrait of
Abraham's submission, this ascetic narrative, lengthened only
by the gloss of 22:14 on the place-name "Adonai-jireh," allows
and even compels the reader to visualize what is recounted,
supply what is withheld, invent the absent dialogue, and
imaginatively build upon every sparse detail.

How can a reader do this, that is, on what authority? If we
came to such a narrative in the context of a familiar body of
literature—characterized, like modern writing, by psychological portraiture—we might praise it for its experiment to do
without psychological specificity, to omit that kind of motivation. But we know little if anything about the literary context
of the *Akedah* story. Basically its text-milieu has to be the rest
of the Bible and rare fragments of ancient Near Eastern literature. In that way the Bible is indeed forced to be its own context. Before we succumb to the habit (impossible to shed
entirely) of psychological probing—conducted on this story in
an exemplary way by Kierkegaard's "Prelude" to *Fear and
Trembling*—it is crucial to define the difference of this narrative *within* its Hebrew context.

Three remarks can be safely made about that difference. Together they emphasize that the "motivation" of the story remains concealed. There is, first of all, an absence of *occasion*—
Abraham is not Jepthah, no oath has been taken, no legal obligation entered into by the father that could lead him toward killing
his child. Then, as I have already mentioned, the dearth of direct
speech suggests a mute or censored layer. Finally, the *Akedah* is
not the act of a jealous or unpredictable monarch-God, the
record of one of his moods. These punishing and dangerous
moods (if that is the right word for them) are—most of the
time—clearly motivated, but here only a "testing" is mentioned,
and anger or retribution does not seem to play a part.

The testing of Abraham *could* have been given a dramatic
context, or justified by what scholars call a motivation-scene.

We find one at the beginning of the Book of Job, and Goethe imitates it by opening his *Faust* with a "Prologue in Heaven." Midrash too supplies such a prologue: the vague time-reference "after these things," which introduces the *Akedah,* is said to suggest a prior episode, an intervention of Satan the Accuser who doubts Abraham's loyalty to God and demands that he be tried. Yet the Bible does not explicitly offer such a scene; we are not as close as Job is to a pagan sky-consultation; there is no formal, paralegal accusation. The result is that what is being tested remains obscure. We might call the obscure object of the testing Abraham's "soul," but it is we who call it such. And it is precisely Abraham's soul, or his introspective state, that we are not given the opportunity to see. Worse, it seems that God Himself cannot discern it: otherwise, why test Abraham? (While the depiction of inner states is unusual in the Bible, it can occur as speech "in the heart": precisely when Abraham is told by God, in Genesis 17, that Sarah will bear a son, "Abraham fell upon his face, and laughed, and said in his heart: 'Shall a child be born unto him that is a hundred years old? and shall Sarah, that is ninety years old, bear?'")

Perhaps we should be grateful for this opaqueness of psyche or soul. It leads us on, draws us not only into the story but into ourselves as readers. Insofar as the *Akedah* generates light rather than darkness, it falls outward onto the traces of a choreographed action that occurs for the first time yet seems already involved in ritual imitation—a sign that there might have been a previous culture, a writing absorbed into this writing. Like Kierkegaard in *Fear and Trembling,* we would like to become Abraham's contemporary, to be present and accompany the steps of this man, to pursue him to the point where it is absolutely clear that such a sacrifice will *not* take place.

Something in us, however, is never sure about the sacrifice not taking place, once its possibility has been suggested. In the great liturgical poem of the medieval author Ephraim of Bonn,

Isaac *is* killed and then resurrected.[3] But Kierkegaard's wish to
enter the scene, as Dante does in his own poem or Keats in *The
Fall of Hyperion*, aims at more than a negative certainty. The
author of *Fear and Trembling* confesses an interest in the
"shudder of the thought," that is, in the psychological impact
on Abraham, Isaac, and Sarah of the realization that a sacrifice
of the only child is being exacted. There is, in Kierkegaard, an
understandable yet morally questionable psychic voyeurism,
which the modern temper encourages.

Kierkegaard wants sight to penetrate inward, to make a
darkness visible. But even if we give up all psychological accen-
tuation, and direct the focus only outward, onto the journey as
a ritual progress, unless we chart the stages and dignify them as
in Christ's ascent to Golgotha, they are a weak ritual. Our mind
has little to grasp except a narrative suspense that is not really a
suspense. What is left is a darkness inside Abraham or inside
God; and the story, absent of any but a divine and obscure motive, inspires empathy rather than knowledge or wisdom.

Ritual process, consequently, is displaced onto the act of
reading. The interpretive quest becomes a frustrated and fascinating repetition—as in Kierkegaard. Reading the Bible is nor-
mally a scanning for (1) ritual or civil law, a motivating precept
that remains partially embedded or obscure, or (2) a mystery,
something not fully present, that must be revealed by adducing
a different place in Scripture or future illumination. If neither
(1) nor (2) obtains, then reading becomes (3) a repetitive and
quasi-ritualized searching of the reader's own conscience for a
clue that would lead through the "imaginative weave" to the
"shudder of the thought." The absence of a motivating law is
precisely what encouraged Christian thought, in its early
polemic against the non-Christian Jews, to exalt Abraham as a
knight of faith: one who believed in God rather than a law,
who was motivated only by faith, *sola fides* (Hebrews 9:17ff).

The drama of the *Akedah,* then, takes place in the narrowest arena, between father and son, father and father, solitary and God. The call that starts it all remains a haunting fact; and where obedience seems to be purest it is also most questionable. A voice out of nowhere orders a murder it calls a sacrifice, and so we wonder whose voice it is, or what psychic drama is involved in hearing voices, including the voice(s) of God.

Few biblical stories are nearer to us than those that involve Abraham. Yet, paradoxically, our intuitive understanding of the tale, our intimacy with it, is frustrated by a limit: the impenetrability of both God's motivation and Abraham's psyche. It is not the supernatural as such that gets in the way; we easily accept, for instance, the point of view that the "men" visiting Abraham could have been angels, or that God should speak directly to Abraham and Sarah, as if occupying the same space. The simplicity of such moments of biblical sublimity had already impressed Longinus in the first century B.C.E. The difficulty lies rather in what Auerbach names the background: it does not light up entirely; a light-source is missing; every illumination, as also in Rembrandt, falls only on a very concrete, particular scene or segment, the rest remains in darkness. The style may stimulate, as Auerbach suggests, our attempts to fill in what is dark or unstated by a scanning technique like Kierkegaard's; but we also come upon a limit that many, after Freud, name the uncanny, and that is defined by him as an effect derived from a repression of the familiar or *heimlich*—when that returns in sublime or sublimated form.

The *Akedah* strangeness almost defeats even Harold Bloom's "will to power" over the text in his and David Rosenberg's *Book of J.* For while Bloom recognizes in its inventiveness the mark of the documentary source called J (for Yahwist) by scholars, the style is clearly that of another documentary source called E (for Elohist) and expresses an unliberated un-

canniness, one still marked by repression. "The shrewd
courage and humanity of Abraham convince me that in the
Akedah the redactors simply eliminated J's text almost completely. . . . [T]here is an extraordinary gap between the Elohis-
tic language and the sublime invention of the story. J's
Abraham would have argued far more tenaciously with Yahweh for his son's life than he did in defense of the inhabitants
of the sinful cities of the plain, and here the revisionists may
have defrauded us of J's uncanny greatness at its height."[4]

What could this familiar element be that has undergone a
repression? It has to do with voice, or voices. The entire business of J and E and P and D, which Bloom seeks to resolve by
his forceful and imaginative intervention, depends on distin-
guishing those voices as styles of writing—not necessarily of
God but certainly of those who present His words in human
transcription (*belashon adam*). The repression can only be, I
will speculate, that each seeks to do God in one voice rather
than many voices, that they feel bound to construct a mono-
theism of the word and present a unitary Torah. The tower of
the Torah is not a Tower of Babel.

In this story, then, and it is a feature that helps to make it exceptional, one becomes aware of a *rhythm* or art of composition that keeps three elements together: the story as plot, as a
compelling sequence of events; a ritual action (a "legomenon"
or legend whose "dromenon" or original mime has fallen
away); and the focus on sacrifice. If the angel of God had called
from heaven to stay Abraham's hand, and it had ended there,
the feeling of closure so satisfying in the story as it stands
would have evaporated. The story is not complete without the
ram's sacrifice, or without a substitution of that kind. The ritual action I refer to is the sense that a programmed script or

internalized sequence is being followed, which makes of the father at once a punctilious, deliberate agent and a sleepwalker. When Isaac raises his voice to ask where the sacrificial animal may be, there is an interruption, a potential challenge; but the ritual is so strong that it absorbs Isaac's question, and makes it part of the script.

This unity of plot, sacrifice, and ritual action, and the sense of closure they jointly evoke, move us toward an essentially literary intuition: how stories develop out of a central, concentrating purpose—a demand that catches and absorbs the mind totally, that shears away all casual, stray, accidental motions of thought. At the same time, this story like any other requires—in order to have narrative extension—a retardation of the climax, one that is always approached (by author as by reader) with conscious or unconscious motive-force. Here that retardation does not aim at creating suspense but opens a limited space for the unexpected, for surprise or plot-reversal. We approach such a possibility—a recognition that could result in a reversal—with Isaac's one question: "Behold the fire and the wood; but where is the lamb for the sacrifice?"

What does this opening, this limited space for the unexpected, suggest? Despite the fact that God is moving toward establishing his nation through Abraham's seed—through the link of the patriarch's only child, his beloved son, "even Isaac"—and despite the fact that the *Akedah* will reaffirm a covenanted outcome, it remains possible that God might settle on *Ishmael,* who is also a child of the promise (Genesis 17) and whose life He has saved in the previous chapter, even as Isaac's is jeopardized in the present one. Is there an unconscious in God, not just in Abraham: a mind that is absent, as well as the totally steadfast mind we are meant to discern?

The reticence of the text, its *hintergründigkeit* (Auerbach), which does not permit us a glimpse into the heart of father or

son, extends to the figure of God, who is called upon to provide the sacrifice; so that Abraham, in the event, speaks
prophetically rather than deceivingly ("God will provide the
sacrifice"). There is a blind side to this text as there is a dark
side to the moon; and though the text does not present itself as
mysterious, it displays what Spiegel calls the "deliberate con-
junction" of several word-plays centering on the root for "to
see," perhaps cognate with "to fear."[5]

The question is indeed: What is seen here, or what is it to see
(into) God? Whether we call the text's reserve a blind or a
clairvoyant fear, the idea of such seeing, such knowledge, elicits
fear. Or, we are allowed to approach the fear of God only
through the medium of a text like this. How this fear or terror
is defined is not itself a mystery. A killing will take place, a
killing "in the family," and which is here represented as a deliberate rather than random act. The text "binds" this recognition
and trauma is avoided. But the Hebrew Bible's reserve also allows the Christian interpreter to claim that just as Abraham
spoke prophetically out of a certain blindness or unknowing-
ness, so does the "Old Testament" as a whole. The light of the
new covenant, it is claimed, leads anagogically "from shadowy
types to truth" (Milton). Kierkegaard too, in his reprise of the
story, makes the truth of trauma emerge. Yet the Christian text
has its own re-veiling: its explicitly central scene of torture and
suffering is converted into gospel, that is, "good news."

In the *Akedah* story the Creation approaches decreation once
more. If Isaac should be offered up, a people (or chosen lineage)
is threatened with extirpation when it has barely been established. Since the cause for this is not explicitly ascribed to the
human agents or the justifiable anger of God, but remains un-
motivated, a fear about, as well as of, God enters. This fear
points to God's unknowable side—unknowable perhaps even to
Himself. But a traumatic recognition of the potential disunity in

God is limited by the story as story: by the voice of a text that holds steady and masters equivocation by its reserve.

---

1. David Weiss Halivni's *Midrash, Mishnah, and Gemara: The Jewish Predilection for Justified Law* (Cambridge: Harvard University Press, 1986) has demonstrated the prevalence of motivated law in Scripture; I am suggesting that stories too, though quietly, can motivate laws or precepts.

2. *Mimesis* (1946), chap. 1.

3. See Shalom Spiegel, *The Last Trial* (New York: Pantheon, 1967).

4. "Introduction" to *Modern Critical Views: The Bible* (New York: Chelsea House, 1987), pp. 8f.

5. Shalom Spiegel, *The Last Trial,* p. 67. See also "Excursus 16: The Land of Moriah," in *The JPS Torah Commentary: Genesis,* commentary by Nahum M. Sarna (Philadelphia: Jewish Publication Society, 1989), 391f.

The Story of
Rebekah

Clarence Major

The hard questions usually
have no simple answers. For me, writing stories is the best
means of dealing with difficult questions of ethics, morality,
and philosophy. In confronting perplexing questions, in my
fiction and poetry, I've achieved an odd kind of success. Often
I have no idea how to formulate the question, let alone the answer, before I struggle with it through the process of writing.
The writing, then, becomes the avenue into the complex nature of the question itself. If I come out of the process with a
clearer sense of the question, and with no answer—which is
more often the case than not—I am satisfied. That's the odd
success, I mean. I stopped, for example, asking, "Who made
me?" "Where'd I come from?" when I was twelve. I stopped
asking, "Is there a God?" by age twenty-one, after which everything, in Gide's words, seemed "down-hill."

Finding life's questions is the business of fiction and poetry.
But it's impossible to separate the writing from the living and
its stories. They are two narrow highways running parallel
through an unclear and unpredictable landscape. I write to

understand my life, and to understand the lives of people who interest me, just as the biblical author might have done. My family, for example, interests me. I want to understand what the stories of their lives meant and mean. And we know that great stories can be parables for our own lives. They serve to show us how long we have been at our best, how the patterns of human behavior don't change all that much, and also how long we've been at our worst. Stories lay out for us possibilities for the future.

In recently rereading Genesis, I dwelled for some time on the brief story of Rebekah. I am aware that a small number of African-Americans have traditionally claimed ancestry in ancient Israel, tracing their lineage back to one of the twelve tribes. I am also aware of the symbolic importance of Jewish biblical stories to the religious feelings of African slaves in the colonies, and the spirituals they forged from the hardship of their lives. But these two facts didn't concern me when I reread the story of Rebekah.

Her story conjured up for me a seedbed of questions about human behavior that I'd been dealing with both in life and in my fiction. Questions regarding the negative aspects of life, such as selfishness, deceit, pettiness, shrewdness, cruelty, evil, complicity in evil doing, materialism, treachery, naturally interest a writer of fiction. So do questions about the positive, such as obedience, goodness, generosity, kindness, honor, trust, suffering, tactfulness, ambition, devout faith, piousness, scrupulousness, the sense of nobility. Rebekah's life calls to mind each of these traits and tendencies. Her story is a story within stories.

Who, then, is Rebekah? Fixed firmly in the mother-line of the family of Abraham, Rebekah is the daughter of Bethuel and Milcah, sister of Laban, wife of Isaac, mother of Esau and Jacob. She is mentioned only in a few brief episodes of Genesis, and only her burial in Abraham's cave, not even her death, is

recorded. But Rebekah's generosity and kindness are demonstrated in the first episode in which she appears. Abraham's servant, Eliezer, on a trip from Canaan to find a wife for Abraham's
youngest son, forty-year-old Isaac, meets her at the Padan
Aram (Aram-Nahariam/northern Mesopotamia) community
well where the family's water is drawn. Though she's wooed
with jewelry, it is probably not the glitter of gold that ultimately wins her over. Rebekah's selfless generosity in this
scene, where she insists on watering all the camels of Eliezer's
caravan, sets the stage for her marriage to Isaac.

Rebekah marries Isaac in his mother's tent (by going to
bed with him) and becomes a devoted wife. Later, while the
couple is on a trip to Gerar, when Isaac tells the Philistines that
Rebekah is his sister to protect her from being seized by them,
Rebekah effectively plays the part of sister. She and Isaac both
obviously believe in the uses of deception in an emergency.
Twenty years later she gives birth to twin sons, Esau and Jacob,
destined from birth to be in conflict with each other. Esau is a
hunter. He's physical. Jacob is spiritual. He's quiet.

Years pass and their father, Isaac, grows old, and blind. One
day Rebekah, probably eavesdropping, overhears her husband
telling his eldest son, Esau, that it is time for an important ritual. But first, Esau must bring his father venison. Isaac plans,
after the ritual of eating the venison, to bestow, according
to Jewish law, the patriarchal blessing of heirship upon his
eldest son. Directing the family bloodline was of the utmost
importance.

But there seem to be some problems with Esau. Rebekah
and her husband believe Esau to be unqualified for a quiet
spiritual life of devotion to God and family, the most desirable
qualities in a son entrusted to carry on the family birthright.
Both parents disapprove of Esau's marriage to a Hittite woman
of Canaan. Overhearing the conversation between Isaac and
Esau, Rebekah hurries to her youngest, and favorite son, Jacob.

She convinces him that he must intercede. By pretending to be Esau, she tells Jacob that he can trick his blind father, and receive the irrevocable blessing, becoming heir. She cooks goat meat and gives it to Jacob. He, taking it in to his father, apparently convinces Isaac that he is Esau, and receives the blessing.

If Rebekah gambles, she loses, because Jacob now has to go away to his mother's birthplace to avoid the wrath of his brother, Esau. And Jacob is gone for twenty years, during which time his life is miserable. Rebekah's scheme to get the heirship for her favorite son ends, ironically, in her loss of his presence for twenty years. But Jacob does marry a woman, Rachel, in the desired family line. It's a bitter victory. And, finally, as the patriarch of his own tribe, Jacob is destined to become the everlasting symbol of the birth of Israel.

Despite the strong symbolism of their stories and the archetypal natures of Rebekah, her husband Isaac, and her twin sons, Esau and Jacob, the few brief episodes containing Rebekah herself spoke to me on a profoundly personal level In some very essential ways, Rebekah reminded me of the hard-working, generous, strong, quietly ambitious, and determined, though relatively powerless, women in my own family, going all the way back to my great-grandmother Rebekah on my father's side.

Every time I teach Jean Toomer's story "Becky," I think about this white great-grandmother about whom so little is known. Toomer's story begins, "Becky was the white woman who had two Negro sons. She's dead. . . ." The story takes place in the backwoods of Georgia in, say, the 1880s or 1890s. In the end Becky's house (built by black and white townsfolk) falls in on her, becoming her tomb. In other words, her neighbors' condescension and grudging generosity eventually help kill her.

My great-grandmother, who was probably also called "Becky" by those who knew her, gave birth to my grandmother, Anna, in 1882 in Oglethorpe County. I can only imagine the pain this white woman had to endure and possible deceit she had to exercise to survive a racist social system that doubly condemned her for having a child out of wedlock and for hav- ing that child by a black man. Her life is an ironic metaphor for and commentary on the absurd myth of racialized color we live by. She gave up the child at birth.

Anna was raised by a black family, the Jacksons. In a culture where 99 percent of the countless thousands of "mixed race" children, before the twentieth century, had white fathers (*not* white mothers), my grandmother Anna was an oddity. Like Rebekah of Genesis, my grandmother too probably had to find subversive ways of giving expression to her own will.

In a sense, such lives—Becky's, my grandmother's, and the story of the biblical Rebekah—are stories about powerlessness. When a powerless person commits an act of wrongdoing, moral and ethical issues swirl around that person like buzzards around a carcass, just as they do around the powerful. But the implications and ramifications are different.

The main point I'm trying to make here is this: Like the biblical Rebekah, a relatively powerless woman, in order to give expression to their legitimate personal, domestic, social, or political concerns, women like Toomer's Becky and women of my great-grandmothers' and grandmothers' generations often were compelled to behave in ways that can be characterized as deceitful, mean-spirited, unscrupulous, or cruel. This is almost certainly the case with the biblical Rebekah, who was up against the power of the patriarchal family or community.

I think understanding such communities and their histories of particulars gives a writer the basis for understanding how powerlessness works. In the communities I grew up in, both in the North and South, I remember parents (but especially mothers) worrying about whom their offspring married. I remember a neighbor and friend of my mother's going to great extremes, but in a covert manner, to try to sabotage her son's affair with a particular girl of whom she, the mother, didn't approve.

Whether or not we have power we can use openly, and because we want things to go our way, we sometimes try to influence the future turn of events by taking certain actions. With her act of deception, Rebekah tries to assert her influence on the future of her family.

But does Rebekah think about the consequences of her action? As a child, I was told to think before acting. Either Rebekah doesn't think about the consequences of her deception, or she weighs the possible outcome against doing nothing and decides to go ahead with her plan anyway, since the possible problems stemming from the deception seem to her far less than the problem of Jacob not receiving *the* blessing. Or, she doesn't care.

Rebekah loves both of her sons, but Jacob is her favorite. In her own judgment, no doubt, she is acting as a good mother when she devises a scheme—derived from her inability to act openly—to give Jacob an advantage over his brother. We all know, as painful as it sometimes is to admit, that parents have favorites.

The difficult question remains: Is it okay to commit an act of wrongdoing in the interest of a perceived good? Rebekah tricked Isaac. In a short story I wrote called "Ten Pecan Pies," a wife (based on my grandmother Ada) tricks her selfish husband into turning over his prized pecans so that she can bake pecan pies as Christmas gifts for the community. Her deception, like Rebekah's, one might argue, was ultimately for a good cause.

But does that *justify* the act? That is one of the difficult questions. Yet before we get to such a hard reckoning, we have to ask: Is Rebekah merely carrying out the wish of her husband? In other words, is she, by taking upon herself the burden of the "evil" act, letting Isaac off the hook? In this paradigm, Rebekah knows her husband so well, and is so obedient, that she saves

him the difficulty of rejecting his oldest son—the rightful in-
heritor—in favor of his youngest, who is clearly her (and secretly his) choice for the position.

If Rebekah's deception is ultimately the act of a loyal, but
powerless, wife, carrying out the will of her husband, then she
is rehabilitated, at least in literary terms, from her role as a vil-
lain. On the other hand, a deterministic reading would leave
one believing that everything that happened was preordained.
Such a reading would also exonerate Rebekah and Jacob of all
wrongdoing. Among my grandmothers and their church
friends, there was a common expression: "Well, honey, it's the
will of God." In other words, they felt powerless to change the
situation in question. That always puzzled me. I couldn't understand how they knew what God was thinking.

Powerless people act in ways that are not always easy to understand. When I was growing up, I could count the times I
saw the women of my own family take responsibilities or bur-
dens upon themselves to protect their menfolk from having to
deal with some unpleasantness. They not only accepted their
place or role in both home and church, but went out of their
way to make life easier for the men. This may have been noble
and selfless, but it was not necessarily right. Ultimately, I think
it was not good for the women or the men.

But these were strong women. Rebekah, like Isaac's mother
Sarah, was a strong home person. Rebekah was the manifestation of Isaac's home. Her sons were who they were culturally
because of her pervasive presence in the home as its defining
agent. In this sense again she reminds me of women in my
own family—my mother, my grandmothers, who helped define for me my culture. I tried to pay tribute to such women in
my novel *Such Was the Season*, which is about a week in the life
of an elderly black woman in Atlanta.

I feel an empathy with such women, which is sometimes
noted in reviews of my fiction and poetry. This identification

with the female perhaps stems from that part of myself that is itself female, as well as perhaps from my growing up in a house full of women. It took courage and tenacity for women like my grandmother Anna to endure. Perhaps I instinctively understood who she was in the face of what she had to do to get through her life.

In the end, do we know who Rebekah is? Rebekah as a virgin girl by the well, who volunteers to water a caravan of ten camels, is the same Rebekah who, many years later, urges her son Jacob to deceive his father. We know that her life has many implications. One is the notion that even from a base of powerlessness, a person can sometimes exert a degree of power. But, as with any human life, the task is to consider the whole life before passing judgment. How do one or two moments of deception—of breaking the rules—fit into a whole life of hospitality, trust, compassion, faith, and generosity?

Ultimately, and when viewed in retrospect, breaking the rules or even breaking the law is not always bad. The serfs of Russia broke the law when they rose up against the ruling class. Rosa Parks broke the law when she refused to move to the back of the bus. Rebekah of Genesis is a good person who breaks the rules. The result is biblical history.

The Story
of Rebekah
as a Mother

Kathleen Norris

On the morning of Holy
Saturday, standing in the chilly chapter house of a monastery, I
once flipped a coin with a young monk to determine how we'd
divide the reading from Genesis, the creation story that would
open the long series of readings at that night's Easter Vigil. He
won the part of God—or the voice of God—and I won the
part of the narrator, which pleased me, because the narrator
has the good lines. That night, standing in a church filled with
over a thousand people, I said the words slowly, "In the beginning . . ." as if I had all the time in the world. And I did. It was
the creation of the world we were saying, and I was surprised
to find suspense in the lines: let there be . . . *and there was,*
God waiting to see, and to call it good.

My recent experience of Genesis has been full of such pleasurable discoveries, and I believe this is because it's been not
only an oral but an aural experience, that of hearing the book
read aloud, straight through, in small installments each

evening during vespers in a monastery choir. In such circumstances, the book came to seem like the family story, and the candles lit for each service a fair substitute for a campfire.

It didn't matter that I'd heard the stories many times before; paying attention always brought new rewards. I quickly came to appreciate, for example, how hearing this ancient literature read aloud tempers the modern bent toward ideological interpretation. When a feminist friend groaned over what he termed "God's ordering Adam to name the animals," I had just heard the story and knew how wrong he was: "So out of the ground the Lord God formed every animal of the field and every bird of the air, and brought them to the man to see what he would call them" (2:19). This implies that God expects to be surprised, and is asking Adam to play along in the continual surprise of creation. While I don't know Hebrew, from what I've read about the language of the creation story, in its original tongue this scene is full of verbal play, little jokes that are intended to convey delight in every aspect of the created world.

Hearing the entire book of Genesis read aloud, I came to revel in being able simply to sit back and listen, letting its words wash over me. And I was reminded over and over that for all its twists and turns, the obvious cut-and-paste job that scholars term interpolation and redaction, it is a remarkably sophisticated narrative. I don't mean that it's fine-tuned and clever in any way that we moderns value—coherent in structure and methodology, precise in terminology, replete with analysis, consistent in its slant. It has too many authors for that, and is too good a story. Much of Genesis is story at its best, full of drama, suspense, and humor, so well-told that it becomes fresh each time we hear it. I doubt that anyone encountering the story of Jacob and Esau, for example, could listen without hanging on every word, longing to know what happens next, and yet half-afraid to find out. Sitting in the monastery choir, I found that hearing *how* it happens, how the whole thing unfolds, was such a pleasure that I was unwilling to forgo it, even for one night.

The story of Jacob's inheritance takes up twelve chapters in the book of Genesis. It might be said to begin with chapter 24, in which Abraham sends a trusted servant to his homeland to find a bride for his son Isaac among his own kin. Coming to a communal well at his destination, the servant has his thoughts laid bare by the narrator as he engages in the sort of deal-making most of us resort to when we find ourselves in need of divine reassurance, or are merely dreaming fated encounters into our everyday lives. Praying, he asks of the Lord, "Let the girl to whom I shall say, 'Please offer your jar that I may drink,' and who shall say, 'Drink, and I will water your camels'—let her be the one whom you have appointed for your servant Isaac" (24:14).

This prayer establishes an expectation in the reader, and also plants a seed of suspense. When a young woman appears with a water jar, we expect that she will be the one, but are not sure. Even though I know the story, hearing it read aloud let that bit of suspense remain a part of the tale's appeal. Of course, the narrator holds us there for only a brief time; soon the girl acts out the drama that Isaac's servant has imagined, speaking the words he has hoped she will say. Her remarkable act of hospitality—she draws water not only for him, but also all ten of his camels, which is no mean physical task—is interpreted by the stranger as a sign of divine providence. That she turns out to be family, Rebekah, the grand-niece of Abraham, signifies not only God's hand in the matter, but is a kind of icing on the cake, a gratifying touch of romance in what is often a brutal book.

I engaged in a bit of daydreaming of my own, as I sat in the monks' choir. I had recently read about a program in Hawaii in which *kupuna* (Hawaiian for "grandparents" or "ancestors") are trained not only in Western psychological methods but also

traditional Hawaiian storytelling for the purposes of counsel-
ing ethnic Hawaiians. Naturally, they begin with genealogy.
"What might first seem like small talk is crucial," one coun-
selor had said. "Where is your family from? Who's your father,
your mother, your *'ohana* [clan]? To Hawaiians that's not
intellectual curiosity, but the entire basis of trust, an unbreak-
able bond." As I listened to Genesis unfold, the repetition of
Rebekah's identity as a member of Abraham's *'ohana* came to
seem not mere repetition but an essential emphasis, a revelation of mysterious but undoubted significance. And I could
not label its importance as "tribal" or "primitive." I am well-
attuned to the family ghosts who appear from one generation
to the next; it generates much of my writing. And living in a
town of 1,600 people, I have come to understand just how
much blood will tell, and how important the interweavings of
families are in understanding the community. Small-town
people, or tribal people for that matter, are much more com-
fortable with a person if they know who their parents were,
their grandparents. I often find that learning a woman's
maiden name is like discovering the solution to a puzzle; it
allows me to place things in proper perspective, to see the
meaning suddenly of otherwise incomprehensible behavior.

In the story of Rebekah, which turns out to be the story of
Jacob and his inheritance, it is her grounding in kinship with
Abraham that makes her later actions so shocking. A small-
town scandal writ large. Fortunately, the narrator of Genesis
does not make us wait as long as I have to let us know that
Isaac and Rebekah do meet and marry with the blessing of her
brother Laban. But it was Rebekah's leave-taking of her family
that most struck me as I heard the tale. Finding herself in a
challenging situation, while she seems to take her social role
for granted, she also lays claim to the unexpected. She does not
flinch at being asked to leave her homeland and enter into
marriage with an unknown kinsman far away. Her family,

wishing her to remain with them for a while, puts the matter to her, but she decides to move on, offering us what may be the most unsentimental leave-taking in literature—*will you go with this man? . . . I will . . .* (24:58). These are the words, the acts of a woman with a strong sense of herself, something that her family recognizes and hopes will lead Rebekah to great things. As she departs, they offer a blessing that echoes the blessing God has given to Abraham, and whose themes will echo again and again throughout the story of Rebekah's son Jacob: "May you, our sister, become thousands of myriads; may your offspring gain possession of the gates of their foes" (24:60). We sense that whatever Rebekah's fate will be, it will be important in the history of her people.

Isaac's response to Rebekah's arrival is psychology in essence, and good psychology at that. In one of the most remarkably compact and suggestive passages in all of Genesis, we are told: "Then Isaac brought her into his mother Sarah's tent. He took Rebekah, and she became his wife; and he loved her. So Isaac was comforted after his mother's death." To end a vespers reading with that passage, to have a night to sleep on it, was a powerful thing. The word "love" seemed unusually potent in this tale of an arranged marriage, and while the portrait of a grieving man finding solace in the company of a bride was as poignant now as when it was first spoken, it left a curious aftertaste, the sense that a beginning so steeped in pain might not bode well for the marriage.

At vespers the next night we took up the brisk genealogy of Genesis 25, but midway through, as soon as we were told, "These are the descendants of Isaac, Abraham's son" (25:19), we were plunged quickly into a vivid rendering of Rebekah's anguish over the children jostling for position in her womb. She cries out, "If it is to be this way, why do I live?" (25:22), and God gives her scant relief, saying, "Two nations are in your womb, and two peoples born of you shall be divided; the one shall be stronger than the other, the elder shall serve the younger" (25:23). Isaac's family story has suddenly metamorphosed into a tale of Rebekah's direct encounter with God, and the listener suspects that Rebekah must act in bold ways to fulfill God's strange prophecy. To the original hearers of the story, people living by the norms of a culture in which the rights of the eldest son were zealously protected to preserve the social order, the prophecy must have seemed troubling indeed—but all the more enticing.

The startling description of the twins' birth—Esau emerging first, ruddy and hairy, with Jacob grabbing his heel—and the careful depiction of their differences as young men—Esau "a skillful hunter, a man of the fields," and Jacob "a quiet man, living in tents" (25:27)—keeps God's prophecy alive for the listener. We also receive an uneasy glimpse of a couple whose marital passion has been transferred to their children: "Isaac loved Esau, because he was fond of game, but Rebekah loved Jacob" (25:28). Nothing prepares us, however, for the story that follows, the almost casual way in which Esau hands over his birthright to his brother. The scene made some of the monks laugh out loud—"Once when Jacob was cooking a stew, Esau came in from the field, and he was famished. Esau said to Jacob, 'Let me eat some of that red stuff, for I am famished'" (25:29). In the monastic tradition, Esau has long been held up as an example of the foolishness of gluttons.

As the long interpolation of chapter 26 intervened—Isaac and Rebekah going to Egypt because of a famine—the question of birthright was left hanging in the air. God had spoken to Rebekah of two nations divided, and it was obvious that the fullness of this story was yet to come. The next night I settled myself in the monks' choir like a child excited over the prospect of a great bedtime story, and in the magnificent narrative of chapter 27, I got it. The telling of Rebekah's acts of subversion, in which she deceives her husband, betrays her eldest son, and makes an accomplice of her beloved youngest, is a sublime example of narrative skill.

Often, listening to Genesis, I came to admire the narrator's gift for telling a terrible story so well that I wanted to listen. Even when I was repulsed—by the hungover Noah cursing his sons, by Abraham binding his son Isaac upon the altar, by Jacob's sons coolly plotting a savage revenge for the rape of their sister Dinah—I found the storyteller's art to be such that the human truths, the psychological implications, remained compelling. I stayed with the story; I wanted it told. In Genesis 27, it was the sensory detail that held me fast: I could picture Isaac's eyes, dimmed with age, and smell the bread and the "savory food" that Rebekah prepares to deceive Isaac, ironically, as we are told several times, cooked just the way Isaac likes it. I could feel the roughness of the animal skins that she places on Jacob's hands and neck, so that Isaac will be convinced that he is Esau, his eldest. I could inhale the earthy scent that causes Isaac to exclaim, again ironically, as he blesses Jacob, that "the smell of my son is like the smell of a field that the Lord has blessed" (27:27).

It was in this chapter, too, that Rebekah's character became dazzlingly clear. When Jacob fears that his father will discover the ruse and curse him, Rebekah says, "Let your curse be on me, my son; only obey my word" (27:13). As the tale rolled along in the monastery choir, I could appreciate a narrator whose rendition of Jacob's visit to a suspicious Isaac is tantalizingly suspenseful, and I was struck also by a new consideration of Rebekah. Here, I thought, is a woman I know. My sister-in-law, for one, sober and responsible, a former Anglican nun who never dreamed that she'd have children, but who told me that when her first child was born and they laid the infant girl on her breast, she had a strong desire to lick her all over, like a mother cat. I thought of my sister, truly gifted as a mother, who might well wish for one of her children, *let your curse be on me,*

165

Kathleen
Norris

if only you are blessed—daring God, or the Fates, to defy her. So far, their fierce mother-love has been good for their children, helping them navigate the hazardous passage of childhood. Where it will lead, God only knows.

When I ponder the mother-child bond, the way some women love their young with all the grace and terrifying strength of a she-bear or a lioness, I recall a pivotal experience of my own late childhood, when on the verge of adolescence I one day realized that I would never be a mother. This was shocking, unthinkable, not a decision or ideological stance—it would be years before I'd hear the word "feminism"—but a revelation of my true self. It came with the quiet certainty of a voice speaking within, possibly God's, bargaining with me, saying, "You will not be a mother, but find another way."

A woman such as Rebekah is disturbing to me: recognizable in the liberating mothering that I've received from my own mother and maternal grandmother—Rebekah, after all, lets Jacob go—but also in the forceful, controlling way in which my paternal grandmother claimed to know "God's plan" for her children. Her youngest son grew up with the burden of knowing that she had, in her words, dedicated him to God while he was still in her womb, and it was many years before she could accept that he would not become a minister like his father. I find much of Rebekah's passion all too comprehensible and laugh at myself as I watch her tragicomical attempts to plan for every contingency lead inexorably to her loss of control over events. She wins the battle—Jacob, and not Esau, is blessed—but it costs her dearly. Her informants—what a household that must have been!—warn her that Esau has threatened to kill Jacob after Isaac dies. Astutely reading her impetuous son—"he is consoling himself by planning to kill you" (27:42), she tells Jacob—she once again asks him "to obey [her] voice" (27:43) and flee to safety with her brother Laban. She will never see Jacob again.

We never learn how Rebekah took her bitter victory. At this point she drops from the narrative, something I hadn't realized, as Genesis continued to unfold in the monastery choir. Jacob's own story came to absorb me, and somehow I think his mother would have approved. First, the wondrous dream of a staircase full of angels, and Jacob's awed response that has become a kind of mantra for me, good to say when the holy manifests itself in unlikely circumstances: "Surely the Lord is in this place—and I did not know it!" (28:16). The narrator gives us a delicious reflection of Rebekah's personality in her brother Laban, who tricks Jacob into marrying Leah. In a mirror-image of Rebekah's plot, Laban sends Leah rather than Rachel into Jacob's tent, ironically in order to preserve the birthright of his eldest daughter. She must have a husband before her younger sister Rachel, the one whom Jacob loves.

But when Jacob returns to his homeland, with Leah and Rachel, their children, servants, and herds, Rebekah is not there. In the long tale of Jacob's tearful reunion with Esau and his years of subsequent wanderings, she is not there. Even at his reunion with his father Isaac at Mamre, where both Isaac and Abraham had lived as aliens, and where the foretelling of Isaac's conception had made Sarah laugh, Rebekah is not mentioned. I regret that we have no portrait of her as a mother-in-law. Would she have been jealous of Rachel, and schemed with Leah against her? Would she have despised both women and tried to reassert her own authority over Jacob? Would the long separation from Jacob have tempered her belief that she could control his destiny? Would she have been humbled, over the years, by recognizing that her own will, which had once seemed so closely interwoven with God's, had necessarily been overshadowed by a divine working out of events beyond her control? The narrator of Genesis does not tell us.

This woman, who first tuned our ear to the powerful patterns of deception and promise, exile and reunion, blessing and curse that recur throughout the tale of Jacob and later his son Joseph, has simply vanished. I longed to hear more of her, even going so far as to imagine her encounter with the narrator, who tells this passionate but unsentimental woman that she has fulfilled her narrative purpose. *"Will you leave the story now?"* the narrator asks, and Rebekah responds, *"I will."*

Rebekah's cunning, bravery, resourcefulness, and passion do live on in Jacob. And after Rachel has died giving birth to Benjamin, the last of Jacob's sons, we are told, "Now the sons of Jacob were twelve" (35:22), which seems the point of the entire tale. God had given Jacob a new name, Israel, but now he has become Israel in more than name, as father of the twelve tribes. And it has all come about because Rebekah, who was supposed to be "safe" as a kinswoman of Abraham, has broken the rules. Sarah laughed. Rebekah's machinations make us laugh, even as we step back a bit, feeling the heat of the fierce maternal passion she displays for her son. Her name does not appear in Genesis again until the end of the book, when an aged Jacob, preparing to die, gives a lengthy blessing to all his sons. *The Collegeville Bible Commentary* describes it as "a rather haphazard collection of sayings about the characteristics and future destiny of the twelve tribes." So be it. It is good to hear Rebekah's name again, and to be told that she had been buried in the cave Abraham had purchased long ago at Machpelah in order to bury Sarah. "There Abraham and his wife Sarah were buried," Jacob says, "there Isaac and his wife Rebekah were buried; and there I buried Leah" (49:31). The scholars tell us that this comes from a priestly source, not from the original narrator of Genesis. No doubt it is useful information to some; I don't much care. I am glad to hear that this woman, whose fierce mother-love has been so well-depicted, has been given her due, placed next to Sarah as the second matriarch of Israel.

The Story of
Rachel

Allegra Goodman

How different the lives in Genesis are from our modern biographies. Today a biography must be at least a thousand pages long to be taken seriously. It squeezes the other books on the shelf; the subject's last name appears in one-inch letters on the spine. A new biography is supposed to be encyclopedic, incorporating newly discovered letters, unpublished manuscripts and diaries, and evidence of previously unknown love affairs. Only then can the volume earn the accolades: "definitive," "monumental," "magisterial," "a landmark." Surely with their towering collections of details, our biographies are the new pyramids. In comparison, the lives in Genesis are elusive mysteries, each linked to the next in the larger history of the Jewish people; none singled out for long. Consider Rachel, Laban's daughter, Jacob's beloved wife, the mother of Joseph and Benjamin. Important though she is, there is no discussion of Rachel's childhood, no analysis of the phases of her life—the Early Years, the Wilderness Years. There is no attempt to fill out Rachel's story with detail. For, of course, there are no details in the modern literary sense, no correspondence or publications. Rachel did not produce a diary, but a nation.

It is difficult to view Rachel apart from the larger narrative and to disentangle her story from Israel's. We first glimpse her arriving with her father's flock, as if in response to Jacob's vision of his future as the beginning of a nation, his dream of radiant expansion and fertility. It is Jacob who sees Rachel, a young woman "fair to look upon" (29:17),[1] and decides her destiny. She will be his wife, and joining to him, will bear his children. The incidents of Rachel's own life, sketched out in Genesis, all take place within the framework of Jacob's journey. But what do we know of Rachel herself? What actions and emotions are her own? And what is the course of her own fleeting biography? She marries Jacob and watches as her sister Leah bears six sons, and Leah's handmaid Bilhah bears two. Rachel's ambition is to bear sons, and her anxiety is that Leah is fertile, while she is not. The bearing of children is a social and political act for Rachel—as for Leah. She will make her mark with her children. But the naming of children is a personal act and a creation of a different kind. Rachel publishes her feelings with her sons' names. When at last her handmaid Zilpah bears Jacob two sons, Rachel names one Dan, from the verb to judge, for "God hath judged me and hath also heard my voice and hath given me a son" (30:6), and the other Naphtali, from the verb to wrestle, for "with mighty wrestlings have I wrestled with my sister and have prevailed" (30:8). The longing is for children, the vision of a future nation is Jacob's, but the naming is Rachel's privilege; and as she names her sons, Rachel makes Jacob's vision her own. Thus she names her first biological child Joseph, connoting increase and prosperity, in expression of her feeling that "God hath taken away my reproach" and in hope that "God will add to me another son" (30:23–24). And in her second childbirth, in the agony of her labor, when the midwife says, "Fear not; for this is also a son" (35:27), Rachel names the child Benoni, the son of my sorrow, the name expressing the moment of pain and desperation, the moment of her death. Jacob changes this name to Benjamin, the son of my right hand, but he uses the structure Rachel began with, "Son of my . . . ," transforming the expression of sorrow into an expression of sustained love.

Jacob loves Rachel more than Leah. The point is made more than once: "he loved Rachel more than Leah" (29:30). His seven years' labor for Rachel "seemed unto him but a few days, for the love he had to her" (29:18). When he is deceived by Laban and wed to Leah instead, Jacob works seven more years for Rachel. Jacob loves Rachel more, but Leah is fertile and Rachel is not. In her rivalry with Leah, Rachel's own voice and ambition emerge. When Leah's son Reuben finds mandrakes in the field and brings them to Leah, Rachel says, "Give me, I pray thee, of thy son's mandrakes" (30:14). Leah retorts, "Is it a small matter that thou hast taken away my husband? and wouldest thou take away my son's mandrakes also?" (30:15), to which Rachel answers, "Therefore he shall lie with thee to-night for thy son's mandrakes" (30:15). The rivalry and the bargain struck recall Jacob's own rivalry with his brother Esau. In his hunger, Esau gives up his birthright to Jacob for the lentils Jacob has cooked. In her longing for the mandrakes and the fertility they promise, Rachel gives up her husband to Leah for the night. But while Esau was possessed by the moment, faint with hunger and incapable of any thought, Rachel's hunger is only for the future and the sons she hopes she will bear. It is she, not Leah, who suggests an exchange for the mandrakes. With the exchange, Rachel plans to establish rather than relinquish her place in history.

In her longing for sons and in the naming of her children, Rachel comes alive in the text. And yet the naming of children is the privilege of the other women in Genesis. A barren womb opened late to childbirth, a rivalry with a second wife are experiences that seem to echo Sarah's. One act of Rachel's, however, seems uniquely hers. It occurs when she and her sister flee with Jacob from Laban's household. Jacob "rose up, and set his sons and his wives upon the camels; and he carried away all his cattle, and all his substance which he had gathered, the cattle of his getting, which he had gathered in Paddan-aram, to go to Isaac his father unto the land of Canaan" (31:17). Jacob takes everything that belongs to him, everything he has worked for. But Rachel, acting alone, uses the opportunity to steal her father's teraphim, his household gods and insignias. This is a remarkable action. The text makes it clear that although he is leaving Laban stealthily, Jacob is taking only the things and the people that rightfully belong to him, for he has worked hard for both (fourteen years for his wives, long years for his flocks). Rachel, however, takes advantage of her father's absence shearing sheep and "stole the teraphim that were her father's" (31:19). Suddenly Jacob's wife is no longer simply a hard-won prize sitting on a camel, waiting to depart with the flocks, pack animals, and all the rest of her husband's substance. She is an independent actor on the scene, taking something for herself.

When Laban catches up with Jacob and berates his son-in-law for leaving and for the loss of the teraphim, the text emphasizes that Jacob knows nothing of Rachel's theft. He protests to Laban, "With whomsoever thou findest thy gods, he shall not live . . . For Jacob knew not that Rachel had stolen them" (31:32). And Rachel, acting alone, hides the teraphim and tricks her father. For she had taken them and "put them in the saddle of the camel, and sat upon them" (31:34). When Laban searches her tent she protects the hiding place under her by declaring she cannot rise before her father, "for the manner of women is upon me" (31:35). Rachel appears suddenly as the central actor on the scene. Jacob and Laban are cast into the background, not acting, but reacting to the confusion she has caused. They become straight-men for her performance. Rachel has brought life into the world and named her children, but this is a creative act of a different kind. When she takes the teraphim she conceals her act and the motives behind it. Rachel's children are her legacy, their names her public confessions and invocations to God, but with the theft and her deception afterward, Rachel creates something else: a lie, a performance, a fiction.

There are many possible explanations for Rachel's trickery. One midrash, pious and monotheistic, suggests that she steals the teraphim to prevent her father from worshiping them. Another darker midrash uses the theft to point to one of those flaws in biblical characters, revealing imperfection even in the greatest examples of humanity. The midrash interprets Rachel's death in childbirth on the way to Ephrath as punishment for her rash act. Rachel is imperfect, her journey incomplete, and so, like Moses, she dies before reaching her people's new dwelling place. Her death on the wayside portends our own state, unready, as yet undeserving of the messianic age. I find in Rachel's theft a moment of intrigue and sheer pleasure within her reticent biography. Here, as she steals her father's teraphim, Rachel acts not merely as wife, daughter, or mother, but as the author of a separate script. The fact that her motives are unclear only seems to enhance Rachel's character; the uncertainty fills her with life. In lacking a clear motive Rachel is granted an interior, a hidden agenda, and an imagination.

I respond to Rachel on several levels. I respond to her as a reader. Her voice, her will, and her quick thinking draw me in. I see her in my mind, bargaining with Leah about the mandrakes, standing with Leah and Jacob in the field and deciding with her sister and husband that it is time for them to leave

Laban and strike out on their own. I see her creeping into her
father's tent and taking the precious teraphim, then hiding
them in her saddle. I take the narrative in Genesis and work at
it in my mind, coloring in the spare outline of Rachel's story
so that I imagine her leaving secretly with her husband's large
household, all the servants, children, and livestock driven together, all leaving as quietly as possible at night so that no one
will see them, so many people and animals disappearing into
the dark. I see Laban searching Jacob's tent and Leah's and at
last Rachel's, where she sits deferential and secretly mocking,
putting her father off with manners. I imagine these scenes
and speculate about them, for, as Erich Auerbach writes of biblical narrative, its spare form, its bare statements where "time
and place are undefined" and "thoughts and feeling remain
unexpressed" all "call for interpretation."[2] The outline of
Rachel's life, the external actions all provoke questions. It does
not matter how much commentary has been written; questioning and speculation are a part of reading this text. The
questions cannot end, because gaps are integral to the story;
the text will never be exhausted, because it can never be filled.

And so I speculate about why Rachel takes the teraphim.
Perhaps Rachel takes and conceals the teraphim from Laban
because she enjoys toying with her father as he has toyed with
her and Leah and Jacob. As she apologizes for rising before
Laban, Rachel invokes custom for her own ends, just as
Laban did before when he rationalized the substitution of
Leah for Rachel with the argument: "It is not so done in our
place, to give the younger before the first-born" (29:26). Or
perhaps, superstitiously, Rachel takes the teraphim with her
not to stop her father's idolatry, but to give her luck on her
journey, and she travels trusting in them, as previously she
had gambled on the power of the mandrakes. Or perhaps she
takes them for another reason altogether—not as idols, but as

tokens of her own lineage and position, so that when she ar-
rives at the household of Jacob's family, she will be received
by Isaac as the daughter of a great house, a woman rich in
her own right. All these possibilities come to mind in the
reading. And with them, Rachel manifests herself as a woman
with many lives, her biography the more valuable because it
is not definitive.

I respond to Rachel as a writer, for she challenges the rule,
not only of the modern biography, but the modern novel. She
is a character who is not developed. Her motives are not established and never analyzed. Imagine Henry James inflicting
himself upon her; imagine the discussion of Rachel's decision
to take the teraphim, the long concealment of the objects, the
burden on her and on Jacob, who does not find out about
them—he could not simply find out. For he would *know,* secretly, and keep the secret—not simply to protect her, but also
silently to rebuke her. Imagine all the action turned inward on
itself. None of that happens in Genesis. The external is shown
and the internal hidden. We must contemplate events on our
own time, not in the text. There are places in Genesis where
the narrative pauses; there are great moments where the inner
life illuminates history, where Isaac weds Rebekah and is comforted for his mother, where Joseph turns away to weep. But
these are moments, not lush discussions, not virtuosic still lifes
of emotion. And so I marvel at the economy of the biblical
text, the movement and perspective of a narrative where the
inner life and the private action startle rather than envelop
the reader.

Rachel is not shaded; there is no attempt to reveal her from
all sides, and by the same token, the narrative does not show
but instead tells the reader what happens. None of the lessons
of fiction or exposition work here. Ideas are merely telegraphed,
threads are left hanging. We have no idea, for example, what

Jacob does when he finds out that Rachel took the teraphim. Does he dispose of them later when he collects from his household "all the foreign gods which were in their hand, and the rings which were in their ears" (35:4)? Rachel's teraphim never reappear. There is a fluidity of detail in the narrative. Details and descriptions are not set up as platforms for future action. They rise up for a moment and then they vanish into the stream. Rachel herself vanishes. The focus shifts, even as her presence and her memory ripple outward in the larger narrative: Jacob remembers her death on the way, and favors Rachel's sons Joseph and Benjamin as he had once favored her. All this counters one kind of biographical and novelistic dogma, a training of the eye on one protagonist, a training to his or her point of view. This focus on one subject, the development of one sensibility is powerful, but it is also simply the fashion. The writer in me enjoys remembering that. For I lose patience with a focus on one character and one point of view. My work always seems to spread itself before me, expanding into the future. One story leads to the next and I find myself writing, not merely about individuals, but about families. *The Family Markowitz* is the name of my new book, and it focuses on different family members, each in turn and tangled up together, the young and the old. It is hard for me to collect my stories in a single book. I already anticipate future events and look ahead to the further adventures of each character. Thus I admire Genesis as a chronicle. I admire both its movement, and the sense of mortality that the movement through time reflects. As I create characters I strive for this, the sense of movement developed so well in the life of Rachel. A sense of the brilliance of a single life as well as its entanglement in the lives of others. A sense of what is unique, mysterious, and irreproducible. A sense of the fleeting moment of each actor on the scene. And, ultimately, a sense of the value of the moment, even as it passes and changes.

Finally, I respond to Rachel as a woman. For she is a great woman, a heroine, fully alive, daughter, wife, and mother, but more than the sum of those roles. Willful, competitive, and also a great adventurer, a traveler moving to a new place, beginning a new life and a new people as well. When I consider Rachel, I think of her as one of those women I would read about as a child in the library of the Women's Studies department where my mother taught. My sister and I would lie on floor cushions in the department lounge reading children's biographies of women—particularly Jewish women, particularly Americans—Henrietta Szold, Rebecca Gratz, Emma Lazarus. This was the 1970s, the age of *Free to Be You and Me,* with its fairy tale about Atalanta, the swift and beautiful runner who outran her suitors and its message that girls could grow into the women they wanted to be, rather than the women they might think they were supposed to be. It was a time when feminists talked without irony about role models for girls. Women in history and women characters in books were presented to us, and sometimes mixed up together in an eclectic iconography. My sister and I had a coloring book, *Great Women Paper Dolls,* which began with Sappho and ended with Golda Meir. I colored Elizabeth I pink and purple; I gave Sappho red hair. We could make the women over; we could fill them with anachronisms. At one level, perhaps the most basic, Rachel is still this kind of figure for me. Neither a historical person nor a character in a book, but the outline of a heroine to be filled and filled again with my own ambition and imagination.

Now I am older—a writer, scholar, wife, and mother of two sons. I consider Rachel and the roles she played. The way she moved within and against her situation. I think more about the limitations and context of her actions. I consider the en as well as the middle of her life, what she could and could not accomplish. I look at it all more carefully. And she is still a heroine for me.

---

1. Biblical quotations are taken from the JPS (1917) translation in J. H. Hertz, ed., *The Pentateuch and Haftorahs: Hebrew Text, English Text, and Commentary,* 2nd ed. (London: Soncino Press, 1979).

2. Erich Auerbach, *Mimesis* (Princeton: Princeton University Press, 1953), p. 11.

The Story of
Jacob's Wrestling
with an Angel

Edward Hirsch

After twenty penitential
years in Mesopotamia, Jacob was hastily returning to Canaan,
land of his birth, where he hoped to be reconciled to his twin
brother Esau, whose birthright and blessing he had taken so
long ago. They would meet face to face. Picture Jacob (Yaakov)
on the horizon—the reflective and wily one, the stealthy intellectual in the family, the cunning younger son grown up and
traveling home like a prosperous tribal chief with his two
wives, Leah and Rachel (one plain and one beautiful), two
maids (Zilpah and Bilhah), eleven sons (the future of Israel itself), a host of servants, and large sturdy flocks of animals. The
procession wound along a route east of the Jordan River. When
Jacob learned Esau was advancing with a force of four hundred
men, he divided everyone and everything into two companies;
he appealed directly to the Lord ("Pray save me from the hand
of my brother"); and he sent ahead gifts of animals in successive droves to try to appease him. Here was one more reminder

180

The Story
of Jacob's
Wrestling
with an
Angel

that Jacob was still guilty and guileful, still fearful of his brother's righteous enmity. The mind boggles at what Esau must have thought as he saw them approaching—one wave after the next, a veritable tide of goats and kids, ewes and rams, nursing camels and their young, cows and bulls, male and female asses. . . .

Jacob set up camp, but that night he suddenly arose and took his family across the ford of the Jabbok. Then he took his possessions and sent them across. He was left alone, and in the darkness a man came and wrestled with him until daybreak. Jacob did not falter, not even when the stranger dislocated his thigh. At daybreak the unknown assailant grew desperate:

> And he said, Let me go, for the day breaketh. And he said, I will not let thee go, except thou bless me.
>
> And he said unto him, What *is* thy name? And he said, Jacob.
>
> And he said, Thy name shall be called no more Jacob, but Israel: for as a prince hast thou power with God and with men, and hast prevailed.
>
> And Jacob asked *him,* and said, Tell *me,* I pray thee, thy name. And he said, Wherefore *is* it *that* thou dost ask after my name? And he blessed him there.
>
> And Jacob called the name of the place Peniel: for I have seen God face to face, and my life is preserved. (King James Version, 32:26–30)

Jacob's encounter with an unknown assailant is a story of majestic strangeness. The Yahwist, who dramatized this episode, perhaps some time around the tenth century B.C.E., was first and foremost not a theologian but a lyricist and a storyteller. As a poet I have returned often, even obsessively, to this jarring scene. I have turned to it for inspiration, but also to try to learn precisely how the Yahwist managed to pack and convey Jacob's encounter with divinity. I have sometimes imagined the Yahwist as a kind of Virgilian guide who could

lead me through the mysteries as I have struggled to dramatize
the *epiphanic* and visionary experiences of others, especially of
writers I care about deeply. This was most evident to me in
writing the poems that went into my fourth collection, *Earthly*
Measures, a book that I wrote between 1988 and 1993. There is
an argument about transcendence in these poems, a quest for
reconciliation to the earth as it is. It was in writing about the
struggle between the immanent and the transcendental that
I returned to the story of Jacob and the angel. For example,
I looked to the Yahwist as a model when I was writing a set
of three pieces—"From a Train," "Unearthly Voices," and
"The Renunciation of Poetry"—about a trip that Hugo von
Hofmannsthal took to Greece in 1908. These lyrics comprise a
modernist triptych that progresses from the moment divinity
asserts itself to the historical instant when the gods turn into a
single God to a time when divinity seeps out of tangible things.
The Yahwist's exemplary imagination also aided me in another
poem, "The Watcher," about Leopardi's experience in Rome in
1823, a lyric in which I tried to substantiate the sense of *nulla*
(or nothingness). And I looked to the Yahwist for guidance as I
wrote "Away from Dogma," a poem that dramatizes Simone
Weil's three mystical contacts with God. Here she is in Assisi:

> She disliked the Miracles in the Gospels.
> She never believed in the mystery of contact,
> here below, between a human being and God.
> She despised popular tales of apparitions.
>
> But that afternoon in Assisi she wandered
> through the abominable Santa Maria degli Angeli
> and happened upon a little marvel of Romanesque
> purity where St. Francis liked to pray.
>
> She was there a short time when something absolute
> and omnivorous, something she neither believed

nor disbelieved, something she understood—
but what was it?—forced her to her knees.

I have tried to learn from the Yahwist how to retain the mystery at the heart of the hieratic confrontation with an unknown
or supernatural force. It may be understood retrospectively
but cannot be naturalized or explained away. Jacob's experience is akin to dreams and visions, yet is presented by the
writer as an event that actually happens. In this regard the author is something of a Kafkaesque dissembler, a purveyor of
the uncanny. Everything is presented as literal. The unknown
assailant knows the etymology of Yaakov's name (heel-holder),
a play on the fact that Jacob had emerged from the womb
grasping the heel of his brother Esau. The stranger also gives
him a farewell-blessing. But this was a common social interac-
tion at the time and didn't require a resort to angels. It was
more unusual for the stranger to rename him "Israel," which
may mean "God-fighter," or "May God protect." Even so, it was
outrageous for Jacob to turn around and claim to have been
face-to-face with God since at the time it was commonly accepted that to see God face-to-face was to die. Jacob saw God
and lived. This revelation was startling, violent, jolting—a leap
of faith. That's how the Yahwist chose to create and define the
ecstatic religious experience. And that's how it would reverber-
ate down through the centuries.

I read Jacob's experience through a literary lens and for me it is
connected to what Wordsworth termed "spots of time." It resembles Virginia Woolf's "moments of being" and James
Joyce's "epiphanies." Such moments are by definition sudden,
unexpected, and apocalyptic. They have a rupturing intensity
that is deep and troubling, even terrifying. They are triggered
by external events but they cannot be anticipated or entirely

explained in rational terms. Indeed, they create a gap or wide
hole in experience as the social world dissolves and the visible
world is usurped. One world is suppressed as another is encountered. The epiphanic moment always marks a crisis point
in a work, a threshold experience. It signals a dramatic turning
point for the protagonist, who is deeply changed by the experience. He may even be so shocked that he emerges from it
claiming a new name, a new identity. Or that he has seen God
face to face.

I think it was when I saw Claude Lorrain's evocative night
landscape in Leningrad in 1973 that I fully understood how indispensable the nocturnal setting is to reading Jacob's story.
Textual scholars have pointed to the great antiquity of a tale
that bears many resemblances to oral sagas in which a hero
struggles against a local river spirit who must be placated or
defeated to obtain a crossing. Folklore abounds with tales of
ghosts and spirits who, like the figure of Hamlet's father, must
slink away before daybreak. The Yahwist uses this tradition to
create a spiritually transforming experience in writing. Psychologically, everything must happen under the eerie cover of
darkness because Jacob's experience is unsightly, epiphanic,
and prophetic, an event out of time. The linear flow and narrative momentum of the overarching story—Jacob's return to his
homeland and reconciliation with his brother—are radically
interrupted; indeed, what we think of as chronological or historical time is completely ruptured on this night of nights. The
event is initiated by two crossings as Jacob sends everyone and
everything to the other side of the tributary, in effect doubly
separating himself from the social realm—the world of famil-
iars, world of possessions. He is enacting a poetic crossing, dis-
possessing himself of his former character. He is now a solitary
traveler left on the edge of a deep gorge. The nocturnal setting
is so crucial because he has moved outside the arena of what
can be apprehended by daylight and has entered the realm of

184

*The Story
of Jacob's
Wrestling
with an
Angel*

the visionary. He has moved from eyesight to vision. The dangerous encounter that follows is the pivotal moment—the turning point—in Jacob's life. The great archaic genius of the Yahwist was to literalize in a human figure the encounter with the Otherworld.

One should keep in mind that Jacob struggles with a man whose identity is unknown to him. He only later takes the stranger to have been a divine emissary. The ambiguity is crucial. It is preemptive to capitalize the word "Man" (as the Living Bible does) and it somehow misses the point to label the section in advance "Jacob Wrestles with God" (as the New International Bible does). A great deal of ink has been spilled trying to identify Jacob's angelic assailant—the candidates include Michael, Gabriel, and many others—but the *elohim* who blesses Jacob resolutely refuses to identify himself. He will not give away his own name. Jack Miles has recently pointed out that virtually all the commentaries follow Jacob's own retrospective interpretation of the event, though the Yahwist leaves tantalizingly open the question of whether or not Jacob ever actually sees the face of the man who disappears at daybreak. And yet there is also an overwhelming warrant in Jacob's entire saga for understanding the struggle as a supernatural encounter. It was foreshadowed in his competitive grappling with Esau in the womb. It resulted in the naming of a nation.

To understand Jacob's encounter I would additionally apply a brilliant rabbinical comment from the *Bereshit Rabba* (chapter one) that Maimonides cites in *Guide for the Perplexed:* "To Abraham, whose prophetic power was great, the angels appeared in the form of men; to Lot, whose prophetic power was weak, they appeared as angels." The prophet's power is greatest when he can read the signs of divinity. One might even say that at Bethel Jacob was still like Lot, a lesser prophet, when he had a dream of angels going up and down a stairway that stretched between earth and heaven. He was something of a stronger prophet at the place he named Mahanaim ("This is God's camp!") when the messengers of the Lord actually met him on the way, though still appearing to him as angels. It was only at Peniel where he was put to the supreme test that he truly became like Abraham, a great visionary, a fully conscious prophet: He wrestled with a man and knew him to be an angel.

I think of Jacob as an agonist of the sublime, a person lamed while seizing the transcendental blessing. His nocturnal encounter was an aspiration for the power of the spirit, a terrifying quest for divine vitality. In the superb first volume of his tetralogy *Joseph and His Brothers,* Thomas Mann describes Jacob's encounter as "A frightful, heavy, highly sensual dream, yet with a certain wild sweetness; no light and fleeting vision that passes and is gone, but a dream of such physical warmth, so dense with actuality, that it left a double legacy of life behind it." The story has such great resonance for poets and prose writers, I think, because writing itself is an encounter with the unknown, a hard struggle with the unsaid, the unsayable. The lyric poem especially is a raid on the mysteries, an attempt to wrestle meaning out of silence. To write is to stand on the edge of a dark gorge guarded by a mysterious stranger. "The written page is no mirror," Edmond Jabès has asserted: "Writing means confronting an unknown face." Jacob may embrace the angel, but for me that embrace must also be agonistic since it is an uncanny confrontation with the unknown, the unknowable. Writing is psychologically dangerous because it means putting one's self at risk. In his poem "Der Angel" Rilke writes of the hands of a being who comes to visit you at night "to test you with a fiercer grip" and "seize you as if they were creating you." They would "break you out of your mould." Like Jacob, writers have always been intent on wresting divinity from demonic hands.

The making of poems is for me both an agonizing and an exhilarating experience. The agony comes because it is so infernally difficult to get something right in words, to substantiate something elusive and intuitive. It's hard to make language answerable to experience—indeed, an experience in and of itself—especially when the experience one is writing about is inchoate or even mystical. But art is also a form of problem solving and I have most often tried to stave off doubts about one's enterprise with an obsessive concentration on what Pound called luminous details. What a pleasure, for example, to saturate myself in Simone Weil's writings, especially in her "Spiritual Autobiography," where she describes her three mystical contacts with God. Absorption is happiness and it makes writing—especially the writing of lyric poems—akin to prayer. Weil called prayer "unmixed attention" and George Herbert described it as "something understood." The exhilaration in writing comes in getting something right, creating a new thing in words, something absorbed and understood.

I can only describe the experience of writing poems metaphorically because it is for me a spiritual as well as a literary enterprise. I'd like to tease out the imaginative implications of that enterprise by associating what happened to Jacob at Peniel with what García Lorca called *"duende."* The *duende* was an Andalusian trickster figure, a sprite something like the Yiddish dybbuk, but in his essay "Play and Theory of the *Duende"* Lorca radically enlarged it into a figure for artistic inspiration. In Lorca's terms the *duende* becomes a demonic presence, a scorched (and scorching) spirit, "a mysterious power which everyone senses and no philosopher explains" (Goethe). "All that has black sounds has *duende,"* Lorca said.

Lorca distinguished among the *duende,* the muse, and the angel, but he thought of the muse as a figure who dictates and prompts from afar, and he considered the angel a dazzling light-filled being who flies overhead. He imagined angels as saintly figures who guide and defend, announce and forewarn. None come to attack. Therefore, he thought, "the true fight is with the *duende.*" Yet Jacob's encounter with an unnamed *elohim* is closer to the struggle Lorca attributed to the *duende.* This struggle is shadowed by mortality. It is anguished, disconsolate, and takes place in a country open to death. Harold Bloom is surprisingly close to this idea when he nominates the Angel of Death as Jacob's unknown antagonist. The *duende* wounds, Lorca said, and fights the creator on the rim of a well, much as the *elohim* marks and permanently injures Jacob on the rim of a gorge. "In the healing of that wound, which never closes," Lorca wrote, "lies the invented, strange qualities of a man's work."

The spirit who wounds and blesses can be taken as a metaphor for the quest to create something lasting from the catastrophe of one's character. Like the ancients, the poet hopes that a new name will bring about a transformation of the self, a new identity. After all, Jacob's new name suggested that he was no longer a supplanter, a heel-holder, but one "who strives with God" (Hosea). The scandal of poetic originality is that the birth of something new is always unsightly; the work comes from a dark, relentless, internal, at times even demented struggle. At times uncertainty itself seems like a literary birthright, unceasing effort a calling. *"Je est un autre,"* Rimbaud said: "I is another." Stealth is required—and courage—when the very self is estranged, especially since one hopes to emerge with a new name, a consoling gift.

I think of writing poetry as a way of forcing a blessing—a creative exuberance, a ringing ecstasy—from the depths of the unknown. The lyric poem is a trope against time, almost a form of religious enthusiasm. Shelley, an apostle of the visionary imagination, said that "Poetry redeems from decay the visitations of the divinity in man." That seems to me an idea worthy of Jacob's sublime encounter. To bring a poem into the world is to feel in a small way in the presence of something sacred, something blessed. Writing is a way of engaging the mysteries. To be like Jacob one must wrestle all night with a stranger and know him to be an angel. One must struggle with an unknown, unnamed fate and then go forth in the morning, wounded, thankful, and refreshed.

The Story
of Judah
and Tamar

Leonard Michaels

The story of Judah and Tamar
tells us very little about Tamar. We never even find out exactly
what happened to her. Did she have sex with Er, the oldest son
of Judah? And what about Judah's next son, Onan, the infa-
mous masturbator—did Tamar have sex with him before he
spilled his seed on the ground? At the end of the story, where
does she go?

From beginning to end Tamar moves amid mysteries, and
yet, before vanishing from the story, she is the most realistic,
practical, and effective character. Her centrality makes it difficult for me to tell the story without imagining what she thinks
and speculating about her motives, but I will try to focus on
the story as it is told, adhering strictly to events until I can no
longer keep Tamar or my personal understanding of her out of
it. She is mysterious, and therefore interesting, so I risk self-
revelation in talking about her, but the story encourages imaginative engagement with Tamar, or what might be called the

desire to know her. After Judah finds out who she is, we are told that he didn't "know" her again. In effect, as the story ends, he abandons her forever to the imagination of others, or to the kind of wonder that inspires erotic projection basic to storytelling, and to knowing the meaning of things generally. The story goes like this:

Judah gives Er, his oldest son, to Tamar to be her husband.

Er is wicked and is slain by God.

Judah gives Onan, his next oldest son, to Tamar as a surrogate for his dead brother.

Onan is wicked and is slain by God.

Judah promises to give Shelah, his next son, to Tamar.

Presumably, Tamar will remain chaste while waiting for Shelah to grow up.

Tamar doesn't wait for Shelah to grow up, and she doesn't remain chaste. She puts on a veil and sits at the crossroad. When Judah comes by and sees Tamar, he thinks she is a prostitute. He propositions her and they agree to terms. Then he has sexual intercourse with her. Thus, Judah impregnates Tamar, the woman he considers a prostitute but who is his daughter-in-law twice over.

When Judah learns that his daughter-in-law is pregnant, he fixes to have her killed. Tamar then proves to Judah that he is the man who made her pregnant.

Judah might have been outraged to think he'd been tricked into having sex with his daughter-in-law, but, according to ancient law, Tamar had done nothing wrong. Indeed, she had done justice to herself in several ways while making certain that the line of Judah is perpetuated, albeit through Judah, not his sons. He couldn't kill the woman who perpetuated his familial line, which is what he wanted in the first place.

Judah reflects on the case and then says Tamar is more "righteous" than he. His remark is legalistic and carries moral overtones. It suggests Judah understands that Tamar has had

enough of his wicked sons. He also understands that Tamar
shouldn't have been told to wait for Shelah to grow up, a tedious prospect, if not merely ridiculous and beneath her dignity. Beyond that, he understands that Tamar didn't expect
Judah ever to give her Shelah after losing his first two sons, but
even if he did, Tamar probably thought Shelah would be as
worthless as the other two.

Considering how she tricked Judah by wearing a veil, he
must have understood that Tamar felt she had been treated like
a prostitute, and that she was acting out for Judah what already
existed in his fantasy life. The veil hid her face, then, but it revealed to Judah what he'd hidden from himself.

Judah must have understood all this, and he was probably
embarrassed, but, being no fool, he learned a good deal from
Tamar, which is what she expected, or she wouldn't have both-
ered to turn him on, so to speak.

When Tamar is in labor and when it is determined that she
is carrying twins, a hand emerges. The midwife ties a red cord
about the wrist to make certain that the firstborn twin will be
recognized, but the other twin emerges first. The twins are
then named and the story ends.

Talking about stories, Samuel Beckett says, "The sun rose,
having no other choice, on the nothing new," by which he means
there is only repetition, one event after another, and there are no
stories. But there was a time when events became stories, and,
like the sun rising again and again, the world was continuously
renewed in stories and invested with meaning. Even the hand
thrusting from Tamar's womb, which seems to thrust out of the
story like an excrescence that doesn't necessarily follow from any
particular event, actually belongs very much to the story. It
makes everything strange and more interesting. It isn't finally
meaningless, or an event that merely happened, but it is rather a
talisman of the wonderful, or a kind of boundary marker in the
metaphysical world of this story that is about to end.

Perhaps Tamar knew from the beginning that Judah was her man. Perhaps Judah knew it, too, but he didn't want to know it until Tamar obliged him to acknowledge—at the very least—that he'd had sex with her. This obligation is partly the subject of my book *Sylvia*, published in 1992, a novelistic account of my first marriage, which is told somewhat in the way of biblical stories.

In my book the narrator says Sylvia reminded him, in the midst of dreadful arguments, that they'd had sex the first night they met. She'd had lovers before him, but the first night mattered greatly. Judah acknowledged that he'd had sex with Tamar, and it mattered greatly. Indeed, Tamar's babies soon enforced a deeper acknowledgment, for the twin boys were re-creations of Judah's two sons—Er and Onan—who were slain by God. If Judah had married Tamar, she would have literally become the stepmother of the dead boys, but Judah didn't want to "know" her again. Nevertheless, in a metaphorical sense, Tamar became the mother of his sons, both dead and alive.

The main point is that Judah had sex with Tamar, and the amazing hand is less a consequence than a manifestation; that is, it didn't follow from anything so much as it issued into being, like a revelation, after the sexual event. When the hand emerged from Tamar's womb a red cord was tied about its wrist, but the baby with the red cord was delivered last, which means first is last and last is first. Precisely this paradox describes Judah's fateful relation to Tamar, for Judah was first—as the father of the slain boys—and also last—as the father of their surrogates, the twins of Tamar.

The moral is that life begins and ends in the relations of a man and a woman, and the sexual act is sacred and therefore not simply conditioned by a moment in time. The biblical story asserts what happened without laboring over meanings, or questions of why it happened, or what motivated the characters. In the bleak assertive style, events become meaningful when they are perceived as sacred stories, just as musical notes become meaningful in relation to other notes in a melody. In this sense of a relation among events, Sylvia would often re- mind me of the first night, as if the first time we had sex were a sacred event. In her eyes it gained grim significance in the years that followed because of my bad behavior.

When Sylvia's husband forgot his sacred commitment to her—established in their first night together—by going off to the movies with a friend, or visiting his mother in the hospital, or sometimes just by going alone to the toilet, there would be a dreadful argument. Her husband would plead with Sylvia to be reasonable, and Sylvia would then feel bitterly hurt and become more unreasonable, and she would say what her ancestor Tamar said to Judah, "But you fucked me," as if her husband, in his plea for reasonableness, desecrated the sacred event, and betrayed the feelings that led her to give herself to him the first night.

He thought she was difficult in the extreme, but he was reluctant to believe she was crazy, and he would say to himself what Judah said: "She hath been more righteous than I."

Sylvia's husband believed, in the face of all evidence to the contrary, that she was "more righteous." For him too the first night marked the beginning of their marriage, or what eventually became the time of their story, though he didn't literally think he was living in any kind of story when Sylvia reproached him.

In writing the book about my marriage, I recalled events and emphasized events as such, without including a great deal of speculation about motivations and feelings. I wanted to reduce my marriage to events so that a story might emerge inevitably from events, the way a story in the Bible seems to tell itself. When I lived amid the events, I didn't ever think they were the events of a story. The marriage was not a story, but only a series of events until the final, tragic event and then the marriage was finished. When thirty years had passed I wrote about what happened, recalling events from memory and from notes in a journal. Only then, as I wrote, something like a story emerged liked the hand from Tamar's womb.

In the New English Bible we're told that Judah's friend lied to him, saying that the woman Judah slept with at the crossroad wasn't just a prostitute, but a sacred prostitute. He lied, according to the translator, in order to make Judah feel better about having slept with her. But in the instant that Judah discovered that he had had sex with his daughter-in-law, he and Tamar entered the imaginary, or the realm of story wherein the sacred appears. Judah and Tamar moved from the emptiness of mere events, or Beckett's modern storyless world of empty repetition, and they entered the sacred, or the metaphysical realm of story. In this realm it is not gratuitous that Tamar, wearing a veil, waited for Judah at the crossroad, for the crossroad has meaning and it represents our blindness to fate. As for Tamar's veil, the sign of prostitution, it also means an invitation to the imaginary or the realm of story where the sexual union of Tamar and Judah leads to justice for Tamar and the redemption of Judah's two lost sons.

Poor Judah. He hoped to control events by thrusting his first two sons upon Tamar and then denying his third son to her. Poor everyone, if the truth were known, but it is never known, only represented in stories that tell us that we gamble with life in our least gesture. The result is old and yet, in stories as in the rising sun, or in the relation of Judah and Tamar, the result is forever renewed. In this spirit I wrote *Sylvia*, trying to tell what had happened so that I could tell what happened.

The Story of
Joseph in Egypt

Francine Prose

As a child I believed that
the story of Joseph was about couture. My favorite page in my
favorite Bible coloring book pictured Joseph being sold into
slavery, still wearing his garish striped coat with its rich opportunities for every crayon in the box and for designing an outfit,
as for a paper doll, a coat for a boy who was pretty in the style
of boys in illustrated Bibles.

Since then I've come to think that Joseph's story is about
being saved by art, being entrapped or threatened and then
freed because one has the power to convert dreams into a plau-
sible narrative about the present and the future: the storyteller's power to reveal what will happen next. By the time I
came to think this, I'd been rescued several times over, first and
most dramatically when the act of writing my first novel liber-
ated me from the prison of Harvard graduate school. Since
then, I've felt as if I've been saved by every word I've written,
freed either from the poorhouse or from the insane asylum
into which I was sure I was headed at that point in my life.

One test of a great story is that each passing decade layers more text between the lines of what is written. Lately, reading the story of Joseph, I understand that it is about the wisdom of seeing one's talents and graces as God-given—unsought blessings for which we can take no credit and over which we have only the slightest control.

If the story of Joseph is about being saved by art, it is also itself highly artful, a shapely novella with subplots, foreshadowing, ellipses, drama, suspense, and stunning reversals all fitting more or less neatly into its profoundly satisfying rags-of-many-colors-to-riches structure. It's a narrative so smoothly executed, so economical and ingenious that a beginning writer could learn how to construct a plot by studying the story's narrative technique and the methods by which it achieves its emotional power. It's a polished, sophisticated work of art roiling with primitive bloodlusts, tribal ambitions, power politics, long-held grudges, and deep emotions. A story of brothers, fathers, and sons, it's an elaborate bildungsroman, with Joseph as the biblical Pip, Julien Sorel, or Young Werther. It's a story of youth, inexperience, experience, and painful education—with all the teaching done by God, and most of it off-stage.

Most of us recognize the story's basic elements: Joseph is sold into Egypt by his brothers, accused of rape by Potiphar's wife, imprisoned, freed when a former jail mate suggests that he can interpret the Pharaoh's dreams, which he does and in the process saves Egypt from a famine that drives his brothers to seek Pharaoh's help—and full circle back to Joseph. We know about the fancy coat given to the favored son, the coat soaked in goat's blood to fake his having been torn apart by a wild beast—an early brilliant prop of the sort later used as a narrative shortcut from the medieval mystery plays to the latest crime thrillers.

But it's the less often remembered details that give the story its drive, the inexorable forward momentum of an Icelandic saga: the repetitions, the parallels, the withheld information, the scenes that take place with slight variations or new con- stellations of characters, the mistaken identities, the conspiracies, the loopy mathematics, the tensions about who knows what, who recognizes whom, how much damage one person can do.

Let us take, for example, the dreams. Most of us have noticed how dreams in fiction often have all the fascination of hearing a colleague's dream recited at punitive length over our morning coffee. Of course there are brilliant dreams in literature: Anna Karenina's nightmare, the visions in Bruno Schulz. Yet most tend to be symbolic versions of a "real" situation meant to alert the reader that a character knows "the truth," but on a subconscious level.

Unlike these implausible or tedious *cauchemars,* the dreams in the story of Joseph are riveting, not so much because of their content, which is mostly simple and rarely includes more than one image or one action per dream (skinny cows eating fat cows) but because of *how much depends on them and their interpretation.* We read the dreams of Joseph, of his two jailmates, and of Pharaoh with intense anticipation because of how we know they will affect the dreamer and those who are listening for the dream's prophetic meaning.

The first dreams that young (at this point, he is seventeen) Joseph tells his brothers when they are working in the fields instantly raises the pressure that will explode in his being thrown in a pit and later sold into Egypt. When Joseph tells his brothers first one dream (that their sheaves of wheat are bowing down to his sheaf) and then another (the sun and moon and stars are bowing down to Joseph) we know, apparently well before he does, just how much his account of his dreams will charm his already-jealous siblings.

Soon enough come the truly chilling dreams, those of the
Pharaoh's baker and chief cupbearer, who are sharing the jail in
which Joseph has been thrown after he is accused of rape by the
wife of his Egyptian master, Potiphar. The baker and cupbearer
have angered Pharaoh for unspecified reasons—just as Joseph
has angered Potiphar, chief of the Pharaoh's guard. Potiphar's
wife has made a pass at Joseph, an advance he rejected; her van-
ity wounded, she cried rape and had Joseph arrested. This is
one among many biblical events that makes you want to hear
the story from the other side. What did Potiphar's wife's think?
One would hate to see this as an exemplary tale about why
women accuse men of rape. In fairness to Joseph, the fact that
he is handsome is mentioned several times, so perhaps his master's wife's helpless attraction represents the downside of the
good looks that make him so beloved by his father and so auto-
matically liked—by Potiphar, Pharaoh, the warden, and
Potiphar's wife. (One subtheme of the Joseph story is that,
within the larger framework of God's plan, the same thing can
function alternately as a blessing and a disaster.)

The baker's and the cupbearer's dreams are especially har-
rowing, because unlike Joseph's dreams, which only make his
brothers hate him, unlike Pharaoh's dreams—the seven fat and
skinny cows, the seven fat and lean ears of grain—which predict seven years of famine that will follow the seven years of
plenty (a famine that, thanks to the warning dream, can be
mitigated and managed)—unlike those dreams, the baker's
dream permits no happy or fortunate resolution.

In the cupbearer's dream, he watches three grapevines grow
buds, then blossoms, then fruit, and he squeezes them into the
Pharaoh's cup—a vision that, Joseph promises, means in three
days he will restored to his former job. But the baker dreams
that he is carrying three baskets of bread on his head and birds
are eating from the basket. With terrible bluntness, Joseph explains that the three baskets signify three days, and that in

three days Pharaoh will hang the baker from a tree and birds
will eat his flesh. (Genesis tactfully refrains from describing
the mood in the prison cell after Joseph reveals that the two
prisoners are headed in different directions.)

As the cupbearer returns to his former life, Joseph asks him
to put in a good word for him with the Pharaoh. So why does
the cupbearer forget about Joseph for two years until he thinks
to recommend him to Pharaoh as an interpreter of dreams?
Perhaps because God knows that Joseph is still a work-in-
progress. He needs two more years in prison to complete the
transformation from a boy strutting in front of his brothers,
from a young man telling the baker that birds soon will be eating his flesh, two more years to become a man who is capable
of mounting an economic and agricultural program that will
save the world as he knows it from famine and starvation.

By the time Joseph appears before Pharaoh, he is thirteen
years older than the youth who so unwisely (if accurately) predicted that his brothers would bow before him. And what has
Joseph learned in the interim, from his encounter with
Potiphar's wife and his time in prison? Humility, faith, moder-
ation, patience, empathy, and good judgment. The thirty-year-
old who tells Pharaoh that it is God—not himself—who will
interpret his dreams is a man who has matured, evolved way
beyond the impetuous boy boasting to his brothers. Recognizing the spirit of God in Joseph, Pharaoh renames him "God
Speaks and He Lives"—and puts him in charge of running his
entire kingdom. From the moment that Joseph appears before
Pharaoh and announces that God will work through him, this
former Canaanite shepherd boy speaks with such authority
that we do not doubt for a moment that he—that God—will
be able to save the country from starvation.

What's most important for us to understand is the sort of
man Joseph has become, because we must know (even as it is
happening) what sort of man is orchestrating the complex

scheme that leads to his reunion with his brothers and his father. And what an astonishing series of scenes whisks us
through the suspenseful plotting that follows the arrival of the
brothers to seek famine relief from Pharaoh!

Though his brothers don't recognize him, Joseph knows
who they are and recalls his dream about them—but *this*
Joseph keeps his mouth shut while they babble on about their
aged father and dead brother and younger brother at home.
(Later, they will tell Jacob that Joseph extracted this information from them.) We can easily imagine what Joseph feels as he
hears this; one attribute of skilled fiction is that we can often
intuit a character's emotions without authorial help. But God
won't let him turn and weep until after he has made his demand that one brother be left behind in Egypt as a hostage
while the others return to Canaan and bring back Benjamin,
Jacob's youngest. What ultimately undermines Joseph's com-
posure is overhearing his brothers agree that his harsh demand
is their long-delayed punishment for what they have done to
their brother, Joseph.

The complicated plot business of the brothers discovering
that they have returned home with the silver they believed
they'd left in Egypt as a sort of deposit, the detail of Pharaoh's
silver chalice hidden and found among Benjamin's things, the
brothers' repetitions of the account of their meeting with
Joseph—all this increases the narrative tension and the emotional pitch, the level of grief and the possibility for grief
(Jacob's dread lest another son, Benjamin, be taken from him)
until the moment when a weeping Joseph reveals his identity
to his brothers and tells them not to blame themselves for the
wrong they did him, because it was all part of God's plan to
save those who would have died in the famine. We need to be
very certain that what Joseph has put his brothers through is
not a protracted scheme of revenge but a course of education:
a brief version of the process by which he himself learned that

his gifts—good looks, authority, the prodigious abilities to interpret dreams and deliver the land from a seven-year-
famine—were all presents from God, gifts with the power to
save human lives . . . beginning with Joseph's own.

Earlier, I said that the act of writing my first novel felt like a
dramatic life-saving rescue. Almost as soon as the novel was
accepted for publication, I took my one-thousand-dollar book
advance, which at that point—this was in 1972—seemed to me
a fortune, and dropped out of the Harvard Ph.D. program in
English, in which I had been a miserably unhappy and barely
adequate student.

Perhaps I should add that the process of writing it felt very
much like a gift. For the first time, I experienced the convic-
tion—those sweetest moments of creation—that the whole
thing was being dictated by some outside source over the
course of a lengthy, often-interrupted but (it seemed to me)
continuous sitting. And now, from a distance of more than
twenty years, it strikes me as less than purely coincidental that
this novel is a story about a rabbi who appears before a king
and saves himself and his people—by telling the long story
within the story that forms the substance of the novel.

Francine
Prose

The Story of
Joseph's
Interpretation of
Dreams

Robert Pinsky

H

ere is the story of the re-
lation between power and imagination, a relation that has not
been slighted by great politicians or great artists.

The story of power in itself tends toward the dignity of epic
or tragedy—a man with a weapon, like David, or with a moral
dilemma, as in the sacrifice of Isaac. We imagine the teller in
the stereotype of bard or chronicler.

In contrast, Joseph's story unfolds in the key of the folk-
tale—a peasant story, a circumstantial and stylized narrative of
famine and gain, brutality and cunning, good looks and good
luck, bad will and deception. This pragmatic, even comic
mode—think of Potiphar's wife, hot for Joseph, still holding
the robe he has slipped out of in fleeing her advances—lacks
the disturbing emotional currents that converge in the tragic
materials of, say, Jacob and Esau.

The teller of the folk-tale, imagined in the stereotype of an elder, a wise man or nurse or grandmother, shares the cunning of her protagonist, that younger son or daughter whose resourcefulness and success reflect the same qualities in the teller. The folk-tale, so often a story of wit and invention, celebrates the worldly power of imagination while deploying that power. To some extent, in this implicit resemblance of narrator and protagonist, it is the tale of tales.

The younger daughter or son by definition lacks power. The elder brothers are stronger, more experienced, and in the tradition of patriarchy closer to that fountainhead of power, the father. Often the youngest is the parental pet or scapegoat—in fairy tales where the doting parent is succeeded by a malign one, both—which is to say, chosen. My onetime colleague Arthur Gold once taught a course called "Genesis as Autobiography," by which he meant the autobiography of the Hebrew people. Chosen, spurned, threatened, downtrodden, mysteriously prevailing through unlikely vicissitudes and unlikely triumphs, the younger son makes, in such an autobiography, an appropriate hero.

He is a favorite, but he is thrown into a pit. He is to be rescued by the most powerful elder brother, but he is not. He is sold into slavery, but he makes a success of it. He is desired sexually, and as a result he is thrown into jail. There he wins friends by his abilities, but they fail him. Though they fail him, he gets out. He thrives, but he is not himself, and takes an Egyptian name. He is restored to his family, but he dissimulates. Though a trickster, he weeps copiously. Though he saves his people, he introduces them into the land of captivity. Though a Jew, he ends as an Egyptian: in the last words of all of Genesis, "they embalmed him, and he was put in a coffin in Egypt."

This picaresque soap opera begins not with Joseph interpreting dreams but with Joseph recounting his own dreams, which are interpreted by others:

Hear, I pray you, this dream which I have dreamed: For behold,
we were binding sheaves in the field, and lo, my sheaf arose, and
also stood upright; and, behold, your sheaves stood round
about, and made obeisance to my sheaf.

The brothers have no trouble interpreting this dream at
all; in fact, they seem to assume that the dreamer knows its
meaning as well as they do. They respond as if he is taunting
them, as the larger animals might respond to Coyote or
Ananzi:

And his brethren said to him, Shalt thou indeed reign over us?
Or shalt thou indeed have dominion over us? And they hated
him yet more for his dreams, and for his words.

The insult to the established order of power is, immediately,
not only repeated but aggrandized:

And he dreamed yet another dream, and told it his brethren,
and said, Behold, I have dreamed a dream more; and behold, the
sun and the moon and the eleven stars made obeisance to me.

And he told it to his father, and to his brethren: and his father
rebuked him, and said unto him, What is this dream that thou
hast dreamed? Shall I and thy mother and thy brethren indeed
come to bow down ourselves to thee to the earth?

Again, it is notable that the matter of interpretation here is
instantaneous, certain, absolute. There is no question. When
the seventeen-year-old narrates these images—"Hear, I pray
you"—to powerful brothers who already dislike him, he is, we
in the audience might feel, asking for trouble. He is innocent,
but is he ingenuous? He challenges power, he challenges it in
the realm of imagination, and power understands the challenge perfectly.

In *Anatomy of Melancholy*, that summary of all the lore of the
Middle Ages, Robert Burton says that the fancy or imagination

is *ratio brutorum,* the reason of brutes, or the closest to reason that they have. Burton says that in human beings it is bound during waking hours by reason and will, but that while we are asleep—as in Goya's great print of the *Sleep of Reason*—it is free, and generates fantastic shapes. Imagination is a vital power, ingredient to the essential formula for the ways of the world.

As to political power, the swift apprehension of Joseph's dreams raises a question about Pharaoh. Is it so difficult to proceed from images of starving cattle and withered ears to the idea of failed crops, to famine and scarcity? I don't think that this element in the tale means that Pharaoh is stupid; if he were, it would diminish the defining instance of Joseph's qualities, and render the event meaningless. Moreover, Pharaoh is treated otherwise as a figure of perspicacity and judgment.

Nor is it quite satisfying to dismiss the transparent quality of the double dream Joseph interprets simply as a stylized or conventional element of the tale, and nothing more than that. The artificial, conventional quality here is an essential component of the answer, but only one component. The graphic, nightmarishly explicit account of the lean cow eating the fat cow, though certainly as stylized and conventional as its aesthetic mode dictates, has a terrible clarity. The second dream, the withered ears of grain devouring the fat ears, emphasizes that clarity. The clarity is so effectively underscored that, for example, a modern rendering of the situation that sees Joseph as a Jewish psychotherapist unraveling the dark coils of the gentile ruler's inner life, encrypted in the darkness of dream, is not merely farcical but wrong.

Pharaoh's plea for interpretation is a stylized, mimetic embodiment of power's need for imagination. The narrative tells us this partly by defying any naturalistic logic:

And it came to pass in the morning that his spirit was troubled; and he sent and called for all the magicians of Egypt, and all thewise men thereof; and Pharaoh told them his dream; but there was none that could interpret them unto Pharaoh.

Robert
Pinsky

We are not, in this kind of narrative, meant to believe that professional magicians and wise men could not connect images of famine with actual famine, or that they could not at least come up with some impressive nonsense or the other. Speechlessness, or a confession that one is at a loss, is not naturalistically accountable.

However, the artificial folk-tale mode is not meaningless or naive. It is expressive, and what it expresses here is the inadequacy of every skill but one. Pharaoh, the man of policy and worldly force, expresses his need of something that governs during the sleep of reason. The wise men and magicians, men of intelligence and supernatural ingenuity, testify further to the need for such an entity, by their silence. Joseph himself refers to that entity; he says it is divine, not in him:

> And Pharaoh said unto Joseph, I have dreamed a dream, and there is none that can interpret it: and I have heard say of thee, that thou canst understand a dream to interpret it.
>
> And Joseph answered Pharaoh, saying, It is not in me; God shall give Pharaoh an answer of peace.

This manifestation, "not in me" yet through me, is what in another terminology we refer to as inspiration. It reflects in the mind of the interpreter the same force that introduced the recounted narrative into the mind of the dreamer. As in Pharaoh asleep, in Joseph awake. In the context of the Hebrew Bible, that force is one of the manifestations of God. In the context of the one who tells the tale of Joseph, it is a force identical to that which guides and constructs the tale.

Thus the storyteller, attractive conduit for the divine force of imagination, is something like a secret double or twin of the younger son: both command a counterforce to the visible, literal force of worldly power. To the extent that Genesis is indeed the autobiography of a people, the Jews become not simply a people of the Word but a people of the Telling, surviving by precisely the quality lacking in the normal run of governors, wise men, and magicians.

This form of insight in Joseph tempers, maybe even contradicts, the notion of an "Old Testament" whose defining characteristic is Judgment, as opposed to Charity. In a literary sense, those last words of Genesis—the end of the beginning—suggest a dark truth enclosed in a formal principle: "embalmed," as Jews are not, Joseph the interpreter, counterpart of the autobiographical narrator, is "put into a coffin in Egypt."

These phrases foreshadow a terrible sequel. Formally, they predict a reversal: the articulate Jewish slave who takes an Egyptian name and brings his people into Egypt will be succeeded in Exodus by an Egyptian aristocrat who makes his name Jewish and leads his people out of Egypt. A mysterious form of vision, the energy of imagination, *not in me* and implicitly *through me,* will drive the protagonist (and agonist) people through tremendous new ordeals and epic contests between inward and outward power.

Above the bardic narrator of epic incidents, and also above the more domestic narrator of folktale, incorporating them, is the writer whose story is the entire autobiography of the Jews. That large story is an account less of judgment than of telling and interpretation, the agon of insight, mysterious power of the seemingly helpless. This is the ever-uncompleted sentence of the People of the Story.

About the
Contributors

GRACE SCHULMAN's books of poetry include *Burn Down the Icons* (1976), *Hemispheres* (1985), and *For That Day Only* (1994). Among her other books is *Marianne Moore: The Poetry of Engagement* (1986). She is poetry editor of *The Nation* and lives in New York City.

Madison Smartt Bell's recent novel, *All Souls Rising,* was a finalist for the National Book Award in 1995. Among his other novels are *Save Me, Joe Louis* (1993) and *Soldier's Joy,* which received the Lillian Smith Award in 1989. His collections of short stories include *Barking Man* (1990). Born in Tennessee, Bell is married to the poet Elizabeth Spires.

Arthur Miller's plays, which have won the Pulitzer Prize and the New York Drama Critics Circle Award, include *All My Sons* (1947), *Death of a Salesman* (1949), *Incident at Vichy* (1964), *The Price* (1968), *The Creation of the World and Other Business* (1972), and, most recently, *Broken Glass* (Penguin, 1994). Among his other books is *Timebends* (1987), a memoir. He lives in Connecticut.

Michael Dorris's books include *A Yellow Raft in Blue Water* (Holt, 1987) and *The Broken Cord* (HarperCollins, 1989), for which he was awarded the National Book Critics Circle Award for nonfiction and the Heartland Prize. His next novel, *Cloud Chamber,* will be published by Scribner in 1997.

Ron Hansen was born in Omaha in 1947. His most recent novels are *Mariette in Ecstasy* (1991) and *Atticus* (1996), both published by HarperCollins. He lives in northern California.

David Mamet was born in Chicago in 1947. Among his plays, which have won the Pulitzer Prize and the Obie Award, are *Glengarry Glen Ross* (1983) and *The Cryptogram* (1995). His novel, *The Village,* was published in 1994. *The Cabin* (1992) and *Make-Believe Town* (Little, Brown, 1996) are his most recent volumes of essays.

David Shapiro's books of poetry include *Lateness* (1977) and *After a Lost Original* (1994), both from The Overlook Press. His most recent critical work was *Mondrian: Flowers* (1992) from Abrams. He won the Zabel Prize from the National Academy for his poetry, and he has been nominated for the National Book Award. Shapiro, who was a concert violinist in his youth, lives in Riverdale, New York.

James Carroll was born in Chicago and raised in Washington, D.C. His novels include *Mortal Friends* (1978), *Prince of Peace* (1984), and *The City Below* (1994). His memoir, *An American Requiem: God, My Father, and the War That Came Between Us,* was published by Houghton Mifflin in 1996. His column appears weekly on the Op-Ed page of the *Boston Globe.*

Alfred Corn's most recent of six books of poems is *Autobiographies* (Viking, 1992). He has also published a volume of essays, *The Metamorphoses of Metaphor* (1987), and is the editor of *Incarnation: Contemporary Writers on the New Testament* (1990). A novel and a book on poetics are being published in 1997. He lives in New York City.

Phillip Lopate's books of personal essays include *Bachelor-hood* (1981) and *Against Joie de Vivre* (1989), and among his books of fiction and poetry are *The Rug Merchant* (1987) and *Confessions of Summer* (1979). He is the editor of *The Art of the Personal Essay* (Anchor, 1994) and a new book series that selects the best essays of the year. A new book of personal essays will appear in 1997.

Norma Rosen's novels include *John and Anzia: An American Romance* and *At the Center*, both of which were reprinted in 1996 by Syracuse University Press. Her collected essays—*Accidents of Influence: Writing as a Woman and a Jew in America* (SUNY Press)—appeared in 1994 and a volume of original midrash on women of the Bible, *Biblical Women Unbound: Counter-Tales*, was published in 1996 by the Jewish Publication Society.

Lore Segal's novels include *Other People's Houses* and *Her First American* (Knopf, 1985), parts of which were published in *The New Yorker*. She has also published two books of biblical translations, *The Book of Adam to Moses* (1987) and *The Story of King Saul and King David* (Schocken, 1991). She lives in New York City.

Geoffrey Hartman was born in Frankfurt, Germany, and is the project director of the Fortunoff Video Archive for Holocaust Testimonies at Yale University. Among his books are *Wordsworth's Poetry* (1964), which won the Christian Gauss Prize, and most recently, *Minor Prophecies: The Literary Essay in the Culture Wars* (Harvard University Press, 1991) and *The Longest Shadow: In the Aftermath of the Holocaust* (Indiana University Press, 1996). His book of poetry, *Akiba's Children*, was published in 1978.

Clarence Major's novels include *Such Was the Season* (1987), *Reflex and Bone Structure* (1975), and *Dirty Bird Blues* (1996), all from Mercury House. He has published nine collections of poetry and edited *The Garden Thrives: Twentieth-Century African-American Poetry* (HarperCollins, 1996). Major lives in Davis, California.

Kathleen Norris was born in Washington, D.C. Her two books of prose, *The Cloister Walk* (1996) and *Dakota: A Spiritual Geography* (1993), have both been bestsellers. Her most recent book of poetry is *Little Girls in Church* (University of Pittsburgh Press, 1995). She lives in Lemmon, South Dakota.

Allegra Goodman was born in Brooklyn and raised in Hawaii. She is a recipient of a Whiting Writer's Award. Her books include *The Family Markowitz* (Farrar, Straus and Giroux, 1996) and *Total Immersion* (HarperCollins, 1989). She lives in Cambridge, Massachusetts.

Edward Hirsch was born in Chicago in 1950. Among his four books of poems, all from Knopf, are *Wild Gratitude* (1986), which won the National Book Critics Circle Award, and *Earthly Measures* (1994). He lives in Houston.

Leonard Michaels was born in New York City. His fiction includes *Going Places, I Would Have Saved Them If I Could* (1975), *The Men's Club* (1981), *Shuffle* (1990), and *Sylvia* (Mercury House, 1992). His books have been nominated for the National Book Award and the National Book Critics Circle Award. He lives in Berkeley, California, and Rome, Italy.

Francine Prose was born in New York in 1947. Among her novels are *Hungry Hearts* (1983), *Bigfoot Dreams* (1986), *Primitive People* (1992), and *Hunters and Gatherers* (Farrar, Straus and Giroux, 1995). She lives in New York City.

Robert Pinsky was born in Long Branch, New Jersey, in 1940. *The Figured Wheel: New and Collected Poems* was published in 1996, and his translation of *The Inferno of Dante* appeared in 1994, both from Farrar, Straus and Giroux. Several volumes of essays have also appeared, including *Poetry and the World* (Ecco Press, 1988). He lives in Newton Corner, Massachusetts.

About the
Editor

DAVID ROSENBERG is a writer, poet, translator, and scholar whose work has been widely praised. He is the translator of the bestselling literary version of Genesis, *The Book of J* (1990), which he coauthored with Harold Bloom, and the winner of the 1992 PEN/Book-of-the-Month Club Prize for *A Poet's Bible,* the only biblical translation to win a major literary award. The former editor-in-chief of the Jewish Publication Society, Rosenberg has also edited a number of well-received literary collections. His most recent collection, *Communion: Contemporary Writers Reveal the Bible in Their Lives* (1996), became a national religion bestseller. Rosenberg has recently completed *The Book of S: Companion to J.* He and his wife, the writer Rhonda Rosenberg, divide their time between New York City and Miami.